Greenwood Press, 1975.
3 3029 00544 0821

942
F994
1975   Fussell   1150
          The English rural
      labourer
                                     c.1

SEP 2 3 1977   CENTRAL

SACRAMENTO PUBLIC LIBRARY
SACRAMENTO, CALIFORNIA

THE ENGLISH
RURAL LABOURER

EIGHTEENTH CENTURY FARM-HOUSE AND YARD
From *The Complete Farmer*, 1793

THE ENGLISH
RURAL LABOURER

HIS HOME, FURNITURE,
CLOTHING & FOOD
FROM
TUDOR TO VICTORIAN TIMES

by

G. E. FUSSELL
F.R.Hist.S.

GREENWOOD PRESS, PUBLISHERS
WESTPORT, CONNECTICUT

B1P. 8 copy
only sep. copy

Library of Congress Cataloging in Publication Data

Fussell, George Edwin, 1889-
  The English rural labourer.

  Reprint of the 1949 ed. published by the Batch-
worth Press, London.
  Bibliography: p.
  Includes index.
  1. Peasantry--Great Britain. I. Title.
HD593.F88 1975   942   75-10212
ISBN 0-8371-8178-X

All rights reserved

Original edition published by Batchworth Press Limited, London.

Originally published in 1949

Reprinted with the permission of The Hamlyn Publishing Group Limited

Reprinted in 1975 by Greenwood Press,
a division of Williamhouse-Regency Inc.

Library of Congress Catalog Card Number 75-10212

ISBN 0-8371-8178-X

Printed in the United States of America

CENTRAL
C . /

CONTENTS

ILLUSTRATIONS

Frontispiece. Farm-yard from *The Complete Farmer,* 1793

PREFACE

AMONG the many lessons the late war has taught is one that everyone has not so much learned as had forced upon them. It does not very much matter how much money one earns if there are no goods on sale to meet it; nor does it matter if the goods are there to be bought but regulations prevent anyone from buying more than a certain quantity of food or clothing in a special length of time.

The rural labourer of earlier days did not suffer from any such modern restrictions; so far as the goods were on the market he could buy them if he earned enough money, but there was not nearly such a variety of goods and of course he did not earn so much money.

Any consideration of what his wages would buy at any period of history becomes unduly complicated because of the different kinds of things that could be bought, and the additional kinds that were added as time passed, and because of the continuous change in the purchasing power of money in relation to particular articles, say a pair of breeches or a pound of beef.

In this study I have avoided references to money either as wages or as the price of goods for those reasons, and I have tried so far as there is any evidence to determine exactly what goods the rural labourer consumed at different times from Tudor to Victorian days. I have tried to show what house-room he occupied; how many beds and chairs and tables he owned; how much and what kind of food he ate, and how long he had to make a pair of boots last or how many petticoats his wife was able to have. If I have been successful I have been able to define the living of the rural labourer in a physical sense throughout the period and have provided a comparison of the kind of life he led at different times within the four centuries, as well as a basis of comparison with the living of towns-people and the landowning and merchant classes about whom so much more is known.

But before proceeding to the body of my work there are facts which it is essential to state in order that the general conditions of life until quite recent times can be understood.

The appearance of the country was very different in the sixteenth century from what it is to-day, or even what it was in 1900. The population in Tudor and Stuart times was so small that very large areas were uninhabited, or practicably so. The bulk of the small population, perhaps four and a half millions in 1600, lived in a broad belt of country lying between the Wash and the Thames on the east and running across England in a south-westerly direction to the Severn, and much less densely towards the west. Even in the east there was a vast area of 750,000 acres of unreclaimed, desolate fen stretching from Peterborough to Cambridge and Bedford. Northwards, there were the wastes of Lincoln Heath, falling down to the Lincolnshire and Yorkshire fens, all undrained and supporting few people. The great forest of Sherwood occupied half of Nottinghamshire. There were great areas of forest in Warwick, Stafford, Shropshire and Chester, and Derbyshire contained large areas of uninhabited waste and forest. Further north still was an empty desolation of moors, hill and mountain stretching to the Scottish border.

The southern counties were little better. A vast area of forest and waste stretched from mid-Berkshire, across Windsor Forest and south to Bisley and Bagshot, and then across country to Hindhead and Thursley common to the North Downs, thence eastwards in a broad belt right into Kent. Much of this area was still unreclaimed until the eighteenth century. Some is still uncultivated to-day. South was the Weald of Sussex and Kent, which was slowly coming into occupation as the forest was cleared, partly by the needs of the iron founders of the Wealden iron industry. The South Downs were still empty, but the coastal belt was cultivated.

The south-west, from South Hampshire, through Dorset, Wiltshire, Somerset, Devon and Cornwall, though the birthplace of the adventurous sea-dogs who played such a great part in our national story, was still full of forest, down and heath, with few houses.

Gloucester, the south and west midlands, too, contained large forests and desolate hills.

Even the neighbourhood of London was full of waste places, the great forest of Epping on the east and the wild stretches of Hounslow Heath on the west.[1]

Life in such an empty land, away from London, was the life of the

[1] see H. C. Darby. *An Historical Geography of England before 1800*, 1936.

frontier; but the Italianate Englishman, who was commonly regarded as a devil incarnate, brought home the new learning, and the scientific age came to birth slowly but grew increasingly rapidly as time went on. Though we must regard many of the highly spiced concoctions that our ancestors ate as an attempt to conceal the defects of badly preserved food, better conditions were developing. And, as in all peasant communities, despite the long hours of arduous toil, there was a merriment among the people that is revealed by our national reputation for being then addicted to singing and dancing and a jocund feasting whenever opportunity and supplies ran together. Feast days were frequent. A contemporary, William Chamberlayne, in his *Anglia Notitia*, 1660, wrote 'the common people will endure long and hard labour in so much that after twelve hours hard work they will go in the evening to football, stock ball, cricket, prison-base, wrestling, cudgel throwing, or some such like vehement exercise for their recreation'.

Most commodities were home-made, or locally made. Clothing almost always was made domestically from local wool, linen or hemp, from locally cured hides and skins of cattle, sheep and pig. Furniture, when not made at home, was the art of the carpenter who also provided the wood-work of the primitive farm implements, and possibly the framing of the houses that were not built of stone. These were the work of local men who were not professional builders, except those who put up the great mansions.[1]

Little money was needed, and little was in circulation, although supplies were increasing all over Europe as the Spaniards brought the precious metals home, or got their stores taken from them on the way by piratical enterprises of other nations. Values in the money sense were unrealisably low, as some of those stated in the text indicate. In fact, money, as we know it, did not exist before late Tudor times.

From the reign of Henry VII, and perhaps more markedly after the transfer of large areas of land following the dissolution of the monasteries and the suppression of the great abbeys, there was a growing and keen desire for improved farming, and for extending the cultivated area. Population, too, was increasing, though only by about a million in a hundred years, as it did between the death of Queen Elizabeth in 1603 and the accession of Queen Anne in 1702.

Later, theories of farming and new crops were brought back to this country by the refugees who accompanied Charles II when he came to

[1] see my *Social and agrarian background of the Pilgrim Fathers* in *Agriculture History*, October, 1933.

the throne, and, although by the 1650's some market gardening was noticeable near London and Sandwich, in Kent, the growing of vegetables and particularly flowers, at least in the gardens of the squirearchy, developed speedily between 1660 and 1700. Prices, too, were rising, and wages were following them. Interest in farming had become so general and so intense that the Royal Society made the first, unfortunately rather abortive, attempt to secure a report from each county on the farming systems it practised.[1]

As in other things, it was in the following period, the Georgian age, that real progress began. Jethro Tull invented a practical drill for sowing seed mechancially, though it did not get itself adopted until about 1760 and then in a small degree. Indeed, it was not until the beginning of the Victorian age that it became at all general. But early in the Georgian age the new cultivated grasses and turnip began to be effectively cultivated, and interest in these crops was greatly stimulated by the publicity given them by 'Turnip' (1st Viscount) Townsend of Raynham. It was the introduction of these crops that enabled the Norfolk four-course husbandry to be developed in north-east Norfolk, where Arthur Young found it flourishing in the late 1760's. Thence it spread over practically the whole of the light lands of the country and much of the heavy, and called for the enclosure of the open arable fields, so that the right of common grazing on the fallow field might be abolished and the fallow crops, the roots and grasses, grown in safety from the grazing animal, which was confined by the new hedgerows and ditches, or fences, or walls, that brought so much of England to its modern appearance of separate fields.

Already by the time of Defoe's tour (1724-26) inroads were being made on the downland for cereal growing, and there in the seventeenth century the introduction of sainfoin as a cultivated fodder crop had helped the sheep farmer and led to the extension of the cultivated area on which cereals could be grown.[2]

It is not the place here to discuss the coming of the so-called industrial revolution, but the inventions in the cotton industry and the steam engine, the transfer of the iron industry from the Weald to the west

[1] see my *Farming methods in the early Stuart period* in *Journal of Modern History*, 1935, and *Pioneer Farming in the late Stuart age* in *Journal R.A.S.E.*, 1940. R. Lennard, *English agriculture under Charles II: The evidence of the Royal Society's Enquiries* in *Economic History Review:* October, 1932.

[2] see my *Animal husbandry in Eighteenth century England* in *Agric. Hist.:* 1937, and *Crop husbandry in eighteenth century England* in *ibid:* 1941 and 1942.

midlands, the movement of population to the nascent industrial cities of the sparsely populated north, all took their birth in the latter half of the eighteenth century. And population was growing. The five and a half millions of 1700 became nine millions at 1801 and ten millions by 1811.

These people all had to be fed, and their eating overtook the increase in the output of cereals, especially wheat, to which public taste was tending, and which in the next period became the only bread stuff of the English people. The immediate effect was that instead of exporting corn, as we had until about 1775, the country began to import it, in small quantities at first, and not every year to an equal degree, but in a gradually increasing amount as the years passed, so that by the time of the French Wars the population was dependent for a part of their bread on imported flour and corn, and that in spite of all the efforts that the farmers and landowners of the day put forth, stimulated as they were by extremely high prices.[1]

By a coincidence a Board of Agriculture was set up at about the time these wars broke out, and it busied itself at once in making a survey of contemporary farming, even as the Ministry of Agriculture did during the most recent war. The Board, in 1792, appointed a 'reporter' for each county whose business it was to prepare a draft report on local practices on a defined plan, so that all the reports on all the counties could be readily compared, and finally analysed to form a complete survey of the country's agricultural practice and the possibilities there were of improving the general standard of farming. These reports were printed and then circulated to the local farmers and landowners for their comments, which were often caustic, and then rewritten, perhaps after another visit to the county by a second reporter, and a revised edition issued. The writers of these reports are referred to in the body of this book as 'the reporters' and I must say that their work has provided a great deal of information on all the divisions of my subject for the period of the Wars, that is as valuable as it is lacking in the same accessible form about other times.

A 'Union' was an amalgamation of parishes to provide a workhouse for the maintenance of the poor, the 'Union Workhouse' in fact.

By the end of these wars Britain's fate in the nineteenth century, the Victorian Age, the Railway Age, the Empire-building Age, was decided. It was inevitable that we should become an industrial people, and, by so much that we were first in the field, Victorian England be-

[1] see my *Grain supply in two wars:* in *Scientific Agriculture* (Canada, 1932).

came the greatest exporting country, the industrial leaders, the financial dictators, and the capitalists who invested in development enterprise all over the world.

Home agriculture at first prospered like other industries. New manures, new ways of draining the land, better methods of livestock breeding, new machines for saving labour, higher yielding crops and new crops—all led to a higher output and a good deal of legislation in aid was passed. Coupled with the demands of the population, which was increasing still more rapidly as time passed, a period of great prosperity was enjoyed during the first forty years of Queen Victoria's reign, but then various causes combined to destroy British farming until the wars of 1914–1918 brought it into necessary prominence again.[1]

It was during the second fifty years of the nineteenth century that the engineer began to invade the farm. The reaping machine followed the seed drill, and many other relatively complicated gadgets, like hayloaders and elevators, were made, but when steam ploughing and cultivating and threshing became general towards the 1880's the age of mechanised farming had really begun.[2]

This is only a rough outline of the general conditions in which the rural labourer lived and had his being, but it will perhaps suffice as a modest background for the chapters that follow. There is a large body of work that will amplify them, much of it so written as to be deservedly popular, and I have provided a short select list of these works at the end of my book.

G. E. F.

February
1949.

[1] see my *Dawn of High Farming in England* in *Agricultural History* 1948, and *High Farming* in *Economic Geography*, 1948, *et seq.*

[2] see my *Steam cultivation in England* in *Engineering*, 30 July and 13 August, 1943.

ACKNOWLEDGEMENTS

Nos. I, IV and VII are reproduced by courtesy of the National Building Record; No. III is the copyright of *Country Life;* Nos. V and VI supplied by the National Building Record are the copyright of Mr. F. H. Crossley and of the Royal Commission on Historical Monuments (England); Nos. XIV, XV and XVII are reproduced by the courtesy of the Royal Institute of British Architects; and Figures I to IV in the text by the courtesy of Messrs. Methuen.

PART ONE
TUDOR AND STUART TIMES (1485–1714)

Mores' *Utopia*, 1515. Dissolution of the lesser monasteries, 1536. Suppression of the greater abbeys (1539), two events which caused the transfer of a large extent of landed property to secular hands. The Bible in English (1538). The Pilgrim Fathers (1620), followed by the Puritan emigration ten years later. Civil War, 1642–6. 'Protectorate' under Cromwell, 1649–60. Years of plague (1655 and 1666), worse than any since the Black Death. Restoration of Charles II, 1660. Bunyan's *Pilgrim's Progress*, 1670. Monmouth's rebellion in the south-west, 1685.

Population of England
1600, estimated at 4½ million. 1700, estimated at 5¼ million.

B

I COTTAGES

IN Tudor and Stuart days nobody bothered very much about the housing of the rural cottager, least of all the man himself. Life was primitive and almost unbelievably hard to modern ideas. Most of the men and many of the women and children spent the greater part of their time in outdoor work, and the cottage was only a place to sleep in and take some meals. True, in the evenings and winter days a good many odd jobs were done indoors, often by the flickering light of the fire, but sleep overcame these people shortly before or after dark, according to the season. Yet there was a need for new cottages arising out of a number of causes.

One of these was the continuous small encroachments on the wastes which were going on slowly but surely almost everywhere in the country, either by license of the manorial courts, or despite those courts, or from sheer indifference on the part of the Lords of the Manors concerned. Each of these encroachments was made by a man who needed some kind of a house built in which to live.

So numerous had these trespassers become by the reign of Edward VI that it was necessary to pass a law to regularize their position. This was the Act of 1549 which, after reciting that 'in divers counties in this realm there have been builded on commons or waste grounds, certain necessary houses with ground under the quantity of three acres . . . enclosed to and with the same and that in some places there is enclosed a garden, orchard or pond out of and in such wastes and grounds which exceed not the quantity of two acres or thereabouts, which doth no hurt, and yet is much commodity to the owner thereof and to the others', secures such portion of land to the occupant of such house or ground, free from any disturbance by the owner of the waste.

Another reason was the beginning of the break-up of the manorial economy when the great households were being disbanded, and the large bands of retainers, who had formerly lived as various kinds of domestics or armed satellites of great men, were forced to seek an independent source of livelihood. Something of the same happened to the great monastic establishments, whose personnel were thrown upon their own resources at the dissolution.

Many of these people doubtless drifted to the towns; others came to form part of the hordes of sturdy rogues and vagrants who figure so largely in contemporary literature and in the modern histories of that day: but it is likely that many of them were absorbed, slowly enough no doubt, in the farming industry, either as squatters spending their poverty-stricken lives on the edges of the wastes and commons, or as day labourers on the village farms, where a new system of producing for a market was slowly coming into action, and where some developments in farming systems were equally slowly being tried out. Although 'subsistence agriculture' was still the basis of English life, industrial crops were coming into use; e.g. flax and hemp in Lincolnshire and elsewhere; madder and saffron in Essex, which supplied the cloth dyers, whose dyes had formerly been imported from abroad. Hops were grown in many places. Rape and coleseed for oil came a little later.

Clearly there was a demand for new houses, and this is confirmed by Government action. Faced with the spectre of desperate poverty wandering everywhere through the land, Elizabeth passed her famous series of Poor Law Acts in restraint of the vagrant and directed towards providing labour and a minimum maintenance for the 'impotent' but deserving. It was with the idea of enabling men to be self dependent, perhaps, that the Statute of 1589 was passed. It ordered that no new cottage should be built unless 4 acres of land were attached to it, nor must more than one family live in one house. No attention is given to the type of accommodation to be provided for the family, but the Government tried by this means to make the cottagers at least partly free from complete dependence upon wages, and to prevent excessive overcrowding.

Unfortunately this excellent measure was impossible to enforce, because it depended upon local good will by all concerned, and there was a complete absence of control over local action by the central government, although some opinion holds otherwise: but Lancashire Quarter Sessions records several cases of violation, and manorial surveys show that cottagers' holdings ranged from 1 acre upwards in Lincolnshire and other counties, while there are references to landless men in contemporary literature. It is not unlikely that most cottagers had a minute area of land surrounding their dwelling, a trifle of garden or such, yet of 1,664 tenants on forty-four manors scattered over more than ten counties, 10 per cent, or 167 cottages and houses, with or without gardens, are enumerated in Surveys that are still in existence.[1] The Customs of the Manor of Aldeburgh in the time of Henry VIII state that a cottage ground was 80 feet every way, but that half a cottage ground (40 feet every way) was sometimes let, while if two tenants lived in one tenement having 'two several Rowmes in the same', each must pay the usual rent for a single cottage. There can be little doubt that Elizabeth's statute did not do away with sub-letting where it was possible, nor did it ensure that a new cottage invariably had the prescribed number of acres attached to it. There were even then some men

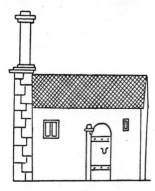

Copyhold House

who depended entirely upon money wages and food given to them by farmers for whom they were working, as well as men in the more satisfactory condition of having the use of plots of land of varying sizes. These, although they had to work for wages upon occasion or to undertake special jobs, such as local cartage, harvest work, winter threshing and work in the woods, had some measure of independence, and just above them in the social scale were those who farmed small areas of 20 acres or little more. These men were farmers, but they were also cottagers living in almost exactly the same kind of house as the so-called free labourer, who formed the bulk of the farm workers at the beginning of the seventeenth century.

Many of the cottages built then are still standing, or were until quite recent times so that the various accommodation they provided is known.

[1] R. H. Tawney, *The Agrarian Problem in the Sixteenth Century* (1912).

In the northern counties, where reclamation of the waste either by legal means, as in parts of the Honour of Clithero, or sporadically by squatters as well, as in Rossendale, and in Sowerby, Soyland and Guisborough in Yorkshire, building varied with the choice of material to hand, but there was a standard of accommodation thought necessary, and provided. The architectural aspect of the cottage has been fully dealt with in *The English Cottage* by Batsford and Fry, and need not detain us unduly here: but a few details are necessary. In a *Survey of lands belonging to the manor of Sheffield* (1611) various farmhouses and buildings are set out. The buildings are described as being of one or more 'baies'. The bay was 16 ft. long and was the space between two 'cruks', the bending beams that joined at the top and stood at each end of the bay to support the roof member. The bays in a house varied according to its grandeur, and there was at least one farmhouse with seven bays on the Sheffield manor. The cottages mentioned are of one bay.

All these cottages were built on the same general plan which has been detailed by S. O. Addy in *The Evolution of the English House* from examples he had seen in West Lancashire at North Meols, at Burscough, at Upper Midhope, near Penistone, and at Hornsea in the East Riding.

One bay would be inconvenient enough for a family to live in, but it could be extended by building additional bays at the ends or extra rooms at the ends or sides. Rooms at the sides, known as outshuts, were outside the bay and not built on cruks. One old house at North Meols had an outshut, 10 ft. by 4 ft., built of wattle and daub. There were no upper rooms, and no ceiling. The living room, presumably the one bay, was known in Lancashire as the house part, in Derby as the house place or house. It had a permanent screen against draught just within the door, against a bench on the inner side, the top being used as a shelf. The mantelpiece was across the whole width of the room. A small outshut entered by a door off one side, opposite the fire-place, was called the buttery and served as a place to keep food and pots. Another door led into two small bedrooms known as chambers and partitioned off halfway up to the roof. Opposite the 'speer' (the permanent draught screen) was a door into another small chamber. All these rooms had clay floors and the house was thatched with rye straw. Another cottage at Burscough, Lancashire, was of one bay but rather larger, and had a little upper room, formerly with access by ladder, and having a small window at the gable end. It even had a small latrine next to the buttery. At Upper Midhope, Penistone was a house, dated 1673, of two bays, the house being 7 ft. 2 in. high, and a steep stair with an open stairhead provided access to the upper floor attics. There was a little round table near the fire for the farmer and his family, while a heavy old table with benches, one of which was fastened to the division partition opposite the fireplace, was used by the servants in husbandry. Addy also states that in his memory there was still a combined house and barn at Hornsea, East, Yorks, the only means of access to the house being through the barn which was built of 'mud'. Similarly a hind's (farm servant in North of England) house was often partly occupied by cattle and partly by the hind and his family, the beasts and human beings being separated only by a wooden partition. Such a house was known as a 'coit'.

Cottages of this general construction, and having much the same

Copyhold House

sort of accommodation, are still to be seen in widely separated parts of the country, e.g. in Gloucestershire, Nottingham, Lincoln and Berkshire. A parson's house at Finmore in Oxfordshire was described in 1634 as a dwelling house of four Bayes, 'sufficiently thatched and in repair'.[1] Indeed most of the buildings in Elizabethan England, even in the 'cities and townes' were, if Harrison's *Description* is accepted 'onlie of timber, for as yet few of the houses of the commonaltie (except here and there in West Country townes) are made of stone'. And there was some doubt in contemporary minds whether brick would hold the heavy roofing timbers used—only would it do so if specially strong piers were put up at the corners, and it took a good many years for innovators like Alderman Metcalf, who built the first brick house in Leeds in 1628, to be imitated. Ralph Thoresby, the topographer, spent some time in 1678 in superintending the building of a chimney in brick.[2]

[1] J. C. Blomefield, *History of Finmere, Oxon.* (1887), p. 78.
[2] D. H. Atkinson, *Ralph Thoresby, the Topographer, his Town and his Times* (1885), pp. 61-2.

For a reason which is unstated and does not at once spring to the mind, Lord Ernle (*The Land and its People*, 1925) suggests that the one bay cruk cottage was displaced in Tudor times by the timber-framed, straw-thatched, two-storey cottage which is found everywhere in the Midland counties, but it seems likely that these houses belong more particularly to the seventeenth century. Ernle was writing of East Hendred, in Berkshire, and in the whole of the Wantage valley such houses are to be seen, but earlier types are not wanting. The one bay house was succinctly described by Bishop Hall and his verse is accepted by Ernle as true of the Elizabethan copyholder. It runs:

> *Of one bay's breadth, Got Wot, a silly cote*
> *Whose thatched spars are furred with sluttish soot,*
> *A whole inch thick, shining like blackmoor's brows*
> *Through smoke that through the headlesse barrel blows:*
> *At his bed's feete feeden his stalled teame,*
> *His swine beneath, his pullen o'er the beame.*

What may have happened there is what happened in Leicestershire. The small farmers were getting better off during the sixteenth century, in the second half of which those who had made money began building half-timbered houses of a size and style formerly unknown in the villages, so that these new houses, cottages though they seem to modern eyes, were really the houses of rich men and not cottagers in the sense appropriated to the word in this work. One example of such a house which contained a hall (house), parlour and kitchen is mentioned in an inventory of goods taken for probate on the death of Robert Smalley, of Galby, Leicestershire, in January, 1559. The hall was the 'house' of the one bay cote, the parlour was furnished with a bed as was then usual, and a small kitchen was at the other end of the 'house'.

Inventories like Smalley's, an example given by C. W. Hoskyns in his study of *The Leicestershire farmer in the sixteenth century*, are very numerous, but only a few of the thousands stored in the Probate Registries have yet been printed. Those that have are often difficult to understand when it comes to deciding how many rooms the goods were stored in, if they are not scheduled by rooms: but they do show that the ordinary farmer of the sixteenth century was very poorly equipped both for house room and furniture. A characteristic Surrey farmhouse, of the cottager type, had a hall, kitchen and chamber just like Smalley in Leicester. A gentleman's residence in Surrey only had a parlour, hall, kitchen and two bedrooms, and it is easy to imagine that if it survived it became a superior cottage in later days.[1] The meagre goods catalogued were contained in similar or even smaller houses in counties so widely separated as Berkshire, Yorkshire and Suffolk, and among them were many of the one-room type.

The Elizabethan chronicler Harrison indicated that in some of the towns in south-west England the houses of his day were built of stone. In the towns they may have been, but the south-west is the home of 'cob', clay mixed with straw used as concrete, and whitewashed or plastered to preserve it from the wet. Similarly, plenty of local stone was readily accessible for building and dry stone-walling. The two materials have probably been used ever since Tudor times in different

Copyhold Cottage

parts of the south-west. Certainly in the sixteenth century and for long after the one room 'cote' or hovel was a commonplace of Cornwall, of Devon, of Somerset and Dorset, where in different places both materials were readily to hand.

Carew of Anthonie in Cornwall,[2] another contemporary, describing cottages used by the few labourers and the small farmers, or the squatters who worked their fingers to the bone in reclaiming small plots of the intractable but extensive waste of that county, says the dwellings had 'walls of earth, low thatched roofs, few partitions, no planchings (i.e. mother earth for a floor) or glasse windows and scarcely any chimnies other than a hole in the wall to let out the smoke'. Even men who might elsewhere have been called yeomen lived in such cottages, slept on straw and a blanket, and possessed furniture which amounted to little more than 'a mazer and a panne or two'. By 1602, when he was writing, these conditions were changed, but only so far as the better off classes were concerned. The poorer classes continued to inhabit these cottages

[1] Uvedale Lambert, *Blechingley, a Parish History* (1921), pp. 513-4.
[2] *Survey of Cornwall* (1602).

with narrow windows deeply set in the walls and corners defended with large jutting stones. It is much more likely that the houses were normally built of wood and clay until at least the end of the reign of Elizabeth; thereafter, and during the seventeenth century and later, the familiar stone built house of the north began to be put up, but the accommodation provided was no more than that to be found in the earlier cruk, wattle and clay building. It was certainly so in the legally enclosed forest lands of Accrington and Rossendale where the tenants of 'the New Hold', made in 1507, so improved their copyhold tenements that 'the process gradually culminated in the erection of substantial stone built houses and buildings of the local yeomanry'.[1]

The dwelling house consisted of two rooms on the ground floor, for a long time, as they did for instance on the verges of Dartmoor, although there the one-room dwellings were built of stone.

In the northern counties, also, stone was used if the proposed building was to be put up conveniently near a quarry or the Roman Wall or a 'dissolved' monastery: but Emily Brontë drew rather heavily on her imagination when she put the date over the door lintel of *Wuthering Heights* as 1500. Otherwise her description is likely to have been correct enough. One stepped straight into the 'house', which usually included both parlour and kitchen, but at Wuthering Heights a later addition had removed the kitchen to another quarter. It was a stone house with a living room with a wide hearth intended to burn peat and logs and a bedroom for the farmer and his wife; probably these were called the 'house' and the 'parlour'. Over these there was a garret or loft open to the roof, and here, after climbing a ladder to get to it, the servants and the children slept. Similar buildings were still the rule in 1720, when the manor court of Hulme Cultram ordered a house of two rooms to be built for a widow under the custom of freebench or widow right.

These were the cottages occupied by the small farmers: 'the poore,' writes a contemporary, 'lived in houses such as a man may build within three or four hours.' These were doubtless the one room 'cotes' so often referred to, which could be built by a squatter and his friends in a moon-lit night so that if smoke issued, not from a chimney, but from a hole in the roof in the morning, there was a somewhat legendary right not to be disturbed.[2] These were put up by ambitious settlers all over the

[1] William Farrer, *The Court Rolls of the Honour of Clitheroe in the County of Lancs.* (1897), iii, p. ix.

[2] R. U. Sayce, *Popular Enclosures and the One-Night House* (1942), in *Coll. Hist. and Arch. Montgomeryshire*, xlviii, Pt. II.

country where the wastes permitted. They were usually built of clay (cob) walls, strengthened by layers of straw and very thick; the roof was thatch and a hole afterwards used as a window was considered sufficient to let the smoke of the first fire escape. It was much like Bishop Hall's 'silly cote', and was to be found so far apart as Cornwall and Cumberland as well as the counties in between. The entertainment provided in such a cottage to a chance traveller is piquantly described by John Taylor, the Water Poet, in James I's reign. Sailing along the south coast he was forced by storms to put in at Hastings where he found a lodging for the night:

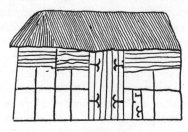

Copyhold Barn

Within a cottage nigh, there dwells a weaver
Who entertain'd as the like was never,
No meat, no drink, no lodging (but the floor)
No stool to sit, no lock upon the door,
No straw to make us litter in the night,
Nor any candlestick to hold the light.[1]

This must have been similar to a Derbyshire cottage of about the same period which was wholly comprised in a single room of clat and clay construction 15 ft. by 13 ft. and 7 ft. high to the wall plates, and thought to be older than the seventeenth century frame built houses. A somewhat similar dwelling was put up on the common waste in another part of the county under license of the manor court in 1676. Such licenses were apparently not unusual in Derbyshire, as might be expected; another had been given to Thos. Saunders in the Manor of Little Chester in 1630.

The village parson, who farmed the glebe and frequently grazed the

[1] *A Discovery by Sea from London to Salisbury* (1623).

churchyard was, despite his education, often little better off than the small farmers and cottagers whose dwellings have so far been our subject. They lived in much the same way as the petty freeholder and cottager proper. At Medmenham, in Buckinghamshire the vicarage house in 1605 consisted of '2 baye built with mudd walls and rough cast and covered with tyle, both bayes being chambered over and boarded, porched and a studdy over that'. This became unfit for habitation (one wonders quite what that implies) and was rebuilt in 1716 as two bays of flint and rubble, each with two floors (what that means is not quite clear from the context) and attics.[1]

In Devon the parsonage of Lynton and Countisbury was, in 1727, just like the 'gentleman's' house in Surrey already mentioned. It had in it three rooms known by the name of a hall, a chamber and a kitchen, the walls part stone and part mud, the floors part paved and part earth.

Enough examples have been given; their repetition would be tedious, and would add little further information. The Tudor and Stuart cottage was clearly a house of scanty convenience to its occupants. At its smallest it contained one room, most probably 16 ft. by 13 ft. and as high or as low as might have been possible to its builders. All over the country the local materials were used in its construction. It may have had 'outshuts', more or less of a lean-to type, to provide sleeping chambers or a larder, and it may have had an attic roughly boarded over the structural beams. Chimney there was often none, at least until it had been added at a later date. Windows without glass would be open spaces, shuttered at night: or possibly provided with horn which let in a dim light.

The yeomen, who were growing richer, had perhaps three rooms, a 'house', a parlour and a chamber, both the latter being used as bedrooms, as was any loft or attic, the latter being achieved by a parlous journey up a ladder. This type was also built of clay (mud) strengthened with straw, or with a timber framing plastered with clay, but as the seventeenth century advanced the stone built house of much the same general dimensions came in, particularly in the north and in the Cotswold country, which was then being settled. Ross in Hereford was remarked in 1693 for its 'famous houses of Slates and Stones'.[2] The two-storey frame and mud building was also becoming more usual in the midland

---

[1] A. H. Plaisted, *The Manor and Parish Records of Medmenham, Bucks.* (1925), p. 324. Ibid., *The Parson and Parish Registers of Medmenham, Bucks.* (1932), p. 375.

[2] *An Histl. Account of Mr. Rogers's three years travels over England and Wales* (1694), p. 101.

counties, and it had perhaps four rooms, two on the ground floor and two above.

'Sanitary arrangements' there were none. Household refuse of all kinds was simply thrown out of the door and left to rot, and the average village must have smelt exceedingly strong. Water supply was from wells, from the local stream, or even from a pond; pollution was a word as yet undreamed of. Survival certainly must have been a struggle even for the fittest in those days. Noses accustomed to the surrounding effluvium from birth were, however, doubtless indifferent to the permanent stench; our ancestors drank little enough water in its natural state, and, unless they went in for swimming, probably required little more than they drank for personal ablution.

II FURNITURE AND CLOTHING

CONTEMPORARY writers, of whom Harrison is the best known
and most quoted, have much to say of the growing luxury of
the wealthier classes, but in the cottages of from one to three
rooms and perhaps a loft or attic over, this growing luxury was not so
evident: although the increasing well-being of the small farmers who
occupied some of them must have led to increased expenditure on
furniture. It was simple enough. 'The farmer has no Flemish tapestry or
Dutch linen; he drinks from bowls, and has but a plain table board and
little plate; his bed is flax, and his curtains of home spun wool; his coat
of frieze or Kendal green; he has two dublets, and not often more than
two servants.'

The evidence of inventories attached to wills obviously deals most
frequently with the more wealthy members of rural society, the nobility
and gentry; but some of the many thousands that still remain to us
were those of the smaller farmers, and occasionally people who could
only have been cottagers in the more restricted sense of the term.

The Surrey farmer, whose cottage was described in the preceding
section, one George Clinch, whose inventory is dated 1637, owned:
Hall—cupboard, table, form, chair and stool. Here presumably meals
were taken, for the kitchen is destitute of such things. It contained a
brass pot, two kettles, shovel, pair of tongs, pothanger, spit and gridiron; Chamber—bedstead, two chests, curtains; Lofts—two bedsteads,
two pair sheets, six pieces pewter, one table-cloth (?) and lumber
including one flockbed and two coverlettes. His apparel and the money
in his purse were worth 10s. together.[1]

Nearly eighty years before, John Crackett died at Bletchingley in the
same county. He lived in exactly the same sized house and his list of
furniture made in 1561 was much the same. It is: Hall—table, two

[1] See *Surrey Archæological Collections* (1910), xxiii, p. 80 *et seq.*

tressels and a forme, chair and two three foted stools, A cobbber, An old painted cloth (tapestry of some sort), Brasse, latten and pewter 'in the howse', quantity not stated; spitts, pothooks, andirons, gridiron. Kitchen—Brewing vessel, trowff and kilderkin (this must have really been a scullery). Chamber—featherbed, four pillows and two boulsters (luxuries condemned by Harrison), three mattresses, four coverlettes, six blankets, fifteen pair sheets (?), four table cloths (?), six napkins, two pillow bers, a stained cloth over the bed, four chests.

Crackett's wardrobe consisted of three cotes, a chamleb Jerkin, freas growne, lether doblet, two pair of hose.

Both of these men were fairly well to do farmers who owned several cows, a plough team of horses, pigs, and Crackett had a small flock of sheep, and they did a little arable farming. They were well above the rank of day labourers.[1]

A Berkshire farmer of much the same status, who died at the time when Latimer was preaching his sermons, left very similar household goods, but his inventory is interesting because it sets out 'his wyves rayment'. It was—a Russett Kyrtell, two Fusten kyrtells, best peticott, olde peticott, a payer of foresleves, a silver pynne, three rebonds, best cappes, a neckercher and five kerchers and other small goods. The man's clothes were—a gowne, a dublet and jacket, two payer hoses, two shirts, a blake sleved cote, A Fryse (frieze), a canvas dublet, a cappe. Neither seems to have had any shoes, or perhaps they were so old as to be valueless.

Robert Littlefield of Padworth, near Aldermaston, in the same county, was a farmer on much the same scale as the two Surrey men. His furniture in 1577 was catalogued as—two flock beds and two bolsters, three pair of sheets, one coverlett, a cubberd, a joyned bedstead, a table and a forme, three cofers and a chest, a joyned stool and a chair, three painted cloths, a brass pot, a kettle, two skillets, tubs, bowls and other lumber worth 4d., three candlesticks, two platters, six pothangers, seven sawcers, one earth dish, a pothanger, gyrd Iren and frying pan, and odd tools.[2]

Anne Green, who owned a moiety, worth £5, of the little tenement she lived in, at Bucklebury, Berks, died in 1640. Her furniture and other possessions only added up to £15 4s. 4d.—including in that £5, a cow and calf, half of 4 acres of vetches and barley, a little stack of hay, apples worth 8s. and wearing apparel 12s.—and consisted only of some

[1] Uvedale Lambert, op. cit.
[2] Mary Sharp, A Record of the Parish of Padworth (1911), p. 131.

brass and pewter, a little poore flocke bed with its appurtenances, bords to lay the bed, three little coffers and one old chest, a table bord, little old cupboard and one old forme. Since Anne's effects included a 'little parcell of woll' it is possible that she did some spinning, although no wheel is included. Her effects are, however, the simplest of any so far catalogued, and although her little tenement may have had two rooms it may only have had one. Her table bord shows that she was using a trestle, and the bed bords that she was not so luxurious as, for instance, Robert Littlefield with his joyned bedstead and candlesticks for lighting his preparations for lying in it, while John Crackett with a featherbed, four pillows and two boulsters slept in luxury indeed. He, however, only had a trestle table in the Hall and he, like most of the others, had a single chair, which was doubtless used only by the master of the house.[1]

Two cottages worth £3 are mentioned in a list of the assets of a manor near Woodstock in Oxfordshire in 1631,[2] and these must have been very tiny places compared even with Anne Green's tenement, the half of which was worth £5; but there were in the county yeomen farmers of exactly the same scale of wealth as those of Surrey and Berkshire, if one example is sufficient to go by. His cottage was the same too; except that his inventory details what was probably little more than a loft, as the Upper Chamber, and this contained: one bedstead, two truckle beds, three flock beds with furniture. Nicholas Higgs, yeoman of Henwick, slept in the bedchamber in one fine bedstead provided with feather bed and furniture. His apartment also had a table, a cupboard, two fine stools and a chest. In the hall were a long table, and frame, one form, one cupboard, two chairs, two fine stools with their lumber. Higgs was evidently fond of fine stools; he had two in his bedroom as well. The second chair in the hall was doubtless for his wife, and it may be surmised the stools were used by his children. There were several pewter things, a flagon, a bowl, a pint pot, a candlestick and dishes, and some of brass, a pot, kettle, skimmer, warming pan, and the usual sparse cooking things, a spit, two frying pans, a grid iron, etc. Linen and holland sheets, a couple of table cloths and four napkins and a holland pillow beare completes the list. In the buttery were five flicks of bacon, barrels, tubs, a salting tub and other lumber. Only two of the inventories so far have included candlesticks; the other people depended upon the humble

[1] A. L. Humphreys, *Bucklebury, a Berkshire Parish* (1932), p. 266.

[2] Herbert Barnett, *Glupton, the History of an Oxfordshire Manor* in *Oxford Record Soc.* (1923), v, p. 25.

I STANE GARTH, BAMPTON, WESTMORLAND

A small 16th or 17th century farm-house, still standing

II SEVENTEENTH CENTURY COTTAGE INTERIOR

—probably stylised. From Charles Knight, *Old England, c.* 1840

III THE RAISED CAUSEWAY AND THE GEORGE INN
LACOCK, WILTS

Probably built in the 16th century. The window frames are modern

rushlight, or even on the firelight for the few short hours of darkness, except in the very depth of winter, before they went to bed. The five flicks of bacon still in store in April in Nicholas Higg's buttery may have been left over because the family had been careful during the winter, or were the accumulation of some years.

There was a disastrous fire at Marlborough, Wiltshire, in 1679,[1] and for some purpose several people compiled lists of their goods which had been destroyed. It was before the days of fire insurance, and can only have been done for some sort of appeal to charity. Not all of the people were husbandmen or their wives, but they were of much the same social status, judging by the money value of their goods, except a tailor who was as well off as the most well-to-do of the farmers mentioned, and had stock and goods worth about £150 in all destroyed.

Deborah Stanmers lost two bedsteads and two beds of flok, two flok bowsters and two fether belows, one pere shets, two bouster cases and three pelo cases. A chaf bed went as well, and five pere of blankets. Her lost cradle rug may have been kept for sentimental purposes; no cradle is mentioned. The kitchen had five boxes, two cofers and one table bord and three pewter dishes. She lost three bibles and other books worth 15s. Can she have been the village schoolmarm? Her clothes were worth £2, about the usual value, and she had two hats burned.

William and Samuel Fowler were definitely shopkeepers and owned a two-tenement house worth £33 8s. They also had three bibles, but there is no distinction between the goods of what could only have been two families. A point of interest is that their inventory is the first so far to mention settles. They had three, and the presence of a small round table and another table board, and two small chairs, seems to show that the same régime existed in tradesmen's cottages as in those of the farmers where labourers lived in—the family ate at the small round table, and the workers at the other table board in the same room, but more distant from the fire.

The rich tailor lost two suits of clothes, a pare of bootes and leather hose. Whether he had another suit on when the fire broke out cannot be said, but it looks as if even a well-to-do man did not have more than three suits, and he may have had only two.

Timothy Chivers, a poor man whose household goods of several sorts were only worth £2 10s., lost a suit of clothes of his own and one

---

[1] *Wilts. Arch. and Nat. Hist. Mag.* (1929), xliv, p. 314 *et seq.*

C

of his wife, which he valued at £3 10s., and £4 10s. worth of linen of all sorts and of lace.

Constant Bennett, who was still poorer, lost one waynskett bed and one standing bedstead, a chest, a coffer, a box, two chairs and one joynstool. Of her clothes only one 'fustian mantl' is mentioned. It is not possible to decide what Dorothy Titcombe was; wife, widow, or spinster, but her clothes, worth £3, are set out in unusual detail. She lost two petycotes, two wascots, one new pair of bodises, and two pair stokins, one pair of shous . . . on riding howed. The rest of her goods were much the same as those of the other people who all lost different quantities of the same sort of things.

There was a large number of wills and inventories in the Probate Registry at Exeter, but few of them have been printed, and the earliest in the *Transactions* of the Devon Association is dated 1715. It is unfortunate that one of the accidents of war has, so I am told, put the rest for ever beyond our reach. One printed by the Royal Institution of Cornwall[1] forms an interesting commentary on Carew's remarks on the paucity of household goods in that county. It is dated 1689, and the husbandman may also have been a miller. His total live and dead stock place him in the same financial category as the more wealthy of those whose wills have already been discussed. He was in the £150 class, like the tailor of Marlborough and some of the farmers. His goods were: one press, one chest, one box, one tableboard, two great stools, two more tableboards, two chairs, three pans, two crocks, one sellet (a salt cellar), eight puter dishes, and he had three beds furnished. This was rather more comfort than Carew allows, but the deceased was a man of substance. Such a collection could, however, only have been housed in a cottage of perhaps the hall, kitchen, parlour (bed-sitting room) type, with a loft or attic above, if there were any upper rooms.

F. C. Hamlyn, in *A History of Morwenstowe after the Restoration*, suggests that the villagers here had only one suit apiece, a pair of skin (? leather) breeches, coat and waistcoat and two shirts, stockings and shoes. The breeches, unless there was an untoward accident, lasted a lifetime. The other things and a hat would have to be renewed from time to time. Such a man's wife would be unlikely to be more sumptuously provided.

Throughout the southern and south-western counties and so far north as Oxford, then, there was a measure of uniformity in the

---

[1] *Journal of the R. Inst. of Cornwall* (1881–3), vii, p. 292.

furniture and clothing of the cottager of the sixteenth and seventeenth centuries, whether he was a labourer for hire, or a small farmer with a holding ranging from 1 acre to perhaps 20 or 25 acres. Again his purse, girdell and wearing apparel ranged in value between about 30s. and £3, rarely less or more. The richer of these small husbandmen, who employed one or two workers, usually shared the kitchen living room with them, but he and his family ate separately at a smaller table near the fire while the workers sat on forms at a bigger table against the wall. The farmer and his wife slept on a feather bed on a joyned bedstead, the servants and children in the upstairs or up-ladder attic on flock beds on bed boards. The farmer may have had a couple of doublets, his wife a couple of petticoats and so on, but their wardrobes were not elaborate. No one, indeed, would expect them to be.

Did their contemporaries in the Midlands and North fare any differently? Not very, if at all! For instance, Robert Child of Paddington in Bedfordshire[1], left goods worth just about £107 in 1582. His home had the usual hall, parlour and kitchen with a buttery and two 'rooms' above furnished as bedrooms. The hall was the living room, furnished with a table board, two forms and one bench, the husbandman's family round table and frame, a cupboard, two andirons and a pair of tongs. The parlour, a bed-sitting room, in which no doubt Child and his wife slept, contained a table board with two forms; square board and frame and forms and two cover stools. He was luxurious with two carpets, three window cloths and four cussons. There was a bedstead and tester without fringe, the latter probably used by one of the children, two feather beds and two feather bolsters, pair blankets, and one coverlet, one andiron, one cupboard. In the kitchen were four brakes (spits), pair racks, three pair pothooks, two pair hangings, seven brass pots two posnets, nine brass pans, four calderons, one gridiron, three frying pans. There were pewter platters and pottingers and other things in the buttery. The two rooms above each had two beds and housed some napery, including three table cloths and four table napkins. Although Child only had about the same head of cattle, horses, sheep and pigs as the men in the south and south-west of the more well-to-do sort, he was more luxuriously provided with household goods, and may have been an example of the increasing comfort demanded by peasant and yeoman families as they grew more wealthy, habits which, as ever, were so strongly condemned by their contemporary, Harrison.

[1] Frederica St. John Orlebar, *The Orlebar Chronicles*, 1553-1733 (1930).

He was one of the type referred to by Hoskyns as growing in numbers in Leicestershire in the last quarter of the sixteenth century, one of the type of richer yeomen who was at that time beginning to build for himself a half-timbered, two-storey, house 'of a size and style previously unknown in the village'. Robert Smalley, already referred to, died at Galby, east of Leicester, and an inventory of his goods is discussed in detail by Hoskyns. In the 'house' was a table board, a form and two stools, two brass pots, two brass pans and a kettle, with two platters and a candlestick 'probably of pewter'. No other things worth enough to list. In the parlour was a bed, bedding and a coffer. No hangings or linen are included, and Hoskyns concludes that these only became common later. The kitchen was sparely furnished with a salting trough, a garner and an ark, a pair of querns (for home-grinding corn) and a few other small utensils. The growing wealth of the husbandman during the century is exemplified by the median value of fifty-eight inventories, taken between 1500 and 1530, which was £14 7s. 11d., and that of 109 made in 1588, which was £46 16s. 8d. from which it will be seen that none of these men was so well off as many of those further south.

A knight, Sir Harry Firebrace, whose biography was written by one of his descendants in 1932, died in 1543. He had a farm at Duffield, Staffordshire. He was no better off than the smaller husbandman of Leicester; his total goods being valued at only £5 15s. 10d. His furniture, though much the same as that of an ordinary husbandman, is remarked by his descendant as scanty. It was two bedsteads with three pairs sheets, two blankets and four coverlets, one aumbry (chest), a meat board (table board no doubt) and two forms, two shelves, two stools and a chair, so it seems that he lived in a two-roomed house, perhaps with a loft above.

The Midland Record Society has published a good number of wills and inventories, but most of these are incomplete, so no precise idea of the comfort or otherwise of the people concerned can be got from them. One is interesting because it does give a more than usually detailed account of the deceased's clothes. One Richard Selman[1] of Aqualate (?) left, in 1558 six jackets and a sleeveless coat worth 10d.; one dublet wolstyd 5s.; one dublet dooskyns 2s.; two flaxen shurt 3s. 4d.; two of hempen 20d.; a pair of bootes and spurres 12d.; a sworde and a dagger 4s.; a sorde gyrdle and a purse 20d.; in all 19s. 2d. worth of clothes.

[1] *Midland Record Soc. Publications* (1899), iii, p. 10.

Further north clothes did not count for so much. William Atkynson of Hayte Field,[1] Woodhouse, in the parish of Hatfield, Yorkshire, died in 1586 and 'all his apparel' was only worth 2s. although it is true that his purse, girdell and more in it came to 2s. more. His total goods, including four beasts, were worth £11 7s. 10d., just about twice as much as those of Sir Harry Firebrace, but it seems unlikely that his cottage had more than two rooms, a kitchen and a 'parlour'. He only had one pair of bedstocks and the bed itself is not mentioned, but he was well off for sheets with two pair of linen, two pair of hemp and one pair of harden, and he had three undescribed mattresses, bolsters, pillowberes and pillows, and two coverlets. Two towéls are an unusual item: while four chests or arks are normal. The brass and pewter in the kitchen are ordinary, but there is an item of 'flesh in the roof' worth 3s. 8d. which was probably bacon or hams or other dried meat.

Robert Todd of Bicker,[2] a Lincolnshire man, died in 1546 worth £21 16s. 8d. His house had a hall, parlour and chamber, the last being used as a store for barley and beans, cheese, ale pots and a milk vessel. The hall and parlour were furnished as living rooms and bedroom, and he was one of the more luxurious husbandmen possessing hangings and cushions in the living room. Otherwise there is nothing unusual in his possession.

The Surtees Society has published a long list of wills and inventories of men of various classes who lived and died in the counties further north. They are very numerous and represent people of all grades of financial strength. A few examples are all that is necessary to show the degree of comfort to be found in their homes.

John Hymers died at Holy Island in 1545, leaving two cows worth 20s. and household goods to the same value, comprising four coverlets, three pairs sheets, two brass pots, ten pewter vessels, two candlesticks and other goods. It is odd that no table forms or bed boards are mentioned. Sir William Bee Clarke, whose address is not given, died in 1551. His clothes, which were fairly numerous, and his furniture seem to have been worth £7 2s. 10d. so he was quite well-to-do. His wardrobe comprised: two gowns, a lined russet froke, one short gown, one clock, one short jacket worsted, cloth jacket, two worsted dubletts, one old, one lether dublett, one old fustian dublett, two short burde-clothes, two pair hose, five tippets, four velvet bonnets, one hat, one hood. What happened to his shoes is not explained. This wardrobe was

---

[1] *Doncaster Gazette*, 21st March, 1842.
[2] *The Reliquary* (1871-2), xii, p. 148 *et seq.*

opulent by the standards of the day, but his furniture was much like that of any ordinary untitled husbandman, except that he owned both linen and harden (hemp) towels and linen and harden napkins; the normal feather bed, bolster, mattress and pillows furnished his sleeping apartment and he had four coverlets, four blankets and one stand bed, one little stool, one awmry (chest), two little chests, two little hangings, one candlestick, five pewter dishes, three sawcers, three pothingers, etc., a frying pan, a roasting iron, a dripping pan.

A fairly large number of wills and inventories relating to Cumberland and Westmorland has been printed in the *Transactions* of the Antiquarian Society for these counties, and the values of the testator's goods and chattels ranged from a pound or two upwards. John Lawe of Yeanwith left cattle and other goods valued, in 1601, at £41 17s. 4d., but the list of his furniture is either incomplete or he had no table, forms or chairs. Cuthbert Orfeur of Pryor Hall, Gent., nearly a century later only left goods estimated to be worth £14 11s. 10d., but here again the inventory is incomplete. Christopher Threlkeld of Melmebie died in 1569 worth £42 1s. 8d. and his furniture is listed as one frying pan, two spits, one kyrsede (?) and two trepetts, pewter vessel, two candlesticks, two pots, two pans, three feather beds with bolsters, two coverings, six worn coverings, two pairs sheets, two pairs worse sheets, two pairs blankets, one counter point, one other bedd covering. Another member of this family, William Threlkeld, Bailiff of Burgh, died worth only £8 10s. in 1564. He owned only four potts, two pans, six pieces pewter and four feather beds, but this must surely be an incomplete list.

It seems a little odd that table boards, forms, bedstocks and other wooden furniture are not mentioned in these inventories, those of the more modestly equipped people. An explanation is a little difficult to find, because these articles of furniture do appear in the inventories of rich men who died worth £200 and upwards. Can it be that the rough and ready nature of life in these wilds three centuries ago was such that the wooden furniture was valueless when it came to be passed on? Was it home-made and so roughly that a table was only a rough plank, and a wooden frame for the bedding was not thought an essential for people who laid on feathers, and who had been doing exhausting work in the open air all day? Perhaps it was only that these things were considered to be so small in value as to be not worth estimating.

One thing emerges very clearly from all this: a large number of the people of the sixteenth and seventeenth centuries were living on the same level of comfort—if that it can be called—although there were the rich and the very rich and powerful who did not fall into this equality. It would be too much to say that it was everywhere the same as in Furness where Norman Penney in *The Household Account Book of Sarah Fell* (1920)[1] has remarked upon 'the paucity of what are called "gentle" families. Practically all the householders were equal, whether they were styled gentlemen or yeomen or husbandmen'.

Many gentlemen, even knights, and yeomen (that indefinite term) were on an equality with husbandmen who had to supplement the profit of their tiny holdings by working for wages at certain seasons of the year, or cottagers who worked for wages all the time. None of them had possessions either in the way of house-room, clothes, or furniture which differed very much from one another except in quantity, and the quantities do not seem to have differed very widely unless the total owned proved worth more than £150 in money of the day. Naturally the cottager living in a one-roomed 'cote' had neither so many 'dubletts' nor so much bedding as the man who lived in what looks like the normal sized cottage or farmhouse of hall, kitchen and parlour, with a buttery, or that more or less, but the best off of these people did possess little refinements unknown to their poorer contemporaries. This is so much to be expected as to be obvious, but these refinements came to little more than a feather bed instead of a flock bed, perhaps a couple of tablecloths and a napkin or two; maybe a candlestick to hold candles made of beeswax rather than the humble rushlight made of mutton fat which glimmered in the 'sawcers' of their poorer contemporaries: no more and no less. Nowhere is any appliance for personal ablution mentioned, and the primitive internal sanitary arrangements are limited to an occasional pewter chamber pot or a close stool. Broadly speaking for the great majority of countrymen there was a similarity, if not an actual equality, in the standard of living, and the very rich and the lesser rich who were trying as ever to live up to their standards, and the man who was trying to rise in the social scale, were so widely removed from the ordinary man in outlook and habit, and were numerically so small a body of persons, that the commercial spirit they were developing had so far come to affect the ordinary man but little. The rise in the cost of living, which was a marked feature of sixteenth century economy, did however make it possible for the gap between rich and poor to grow wider. The small freeholder and the wage earner in a rising market, in which they sold little or nothing but

[1] p. xiii.

their occasional or continuous labour, got little chance of saving; the more well-to-do, as always in such circumstances, grew steadily better off, although as always some of them failed by unwise speculation. There was, however, many a Tony Lumpkin among the small squires a century later, and many a Parson Trulliber and Vicar of Wakefield.

III FOOD

I HAVE already said that life was unbelievably hard in the sixteenth and seventeenth centuries; to that must be added the fact that the shadow of the possibility of famine blackened everybody's life. The point is emphasized by R. H. Tawney in *The Agrarian Problem in the Sixteenth Century* in these words. 'The sixteenth century was poor with a poverty no industrial community can understand, the poverty of the colonist and the peasant. It lived in terror of floods and bad harvests and disease, of plague, pestilence and famine. . . . Yet (and we do not forget the black page of the early Poor Law) it was possible for men who by our standards would be called poor to exercise that control over the conditions of their lives which is the essence of freedom, and which in most modern communities is too expensive a privilege to be enjoyed by more than comparatively few.' Such a measure of control as our cottagers, labourer or small husbandman, could effect was, however, strictly limited by the physical conditions of food production, the soil they worked on, and the vagaries of climate they had to contend with, circumstances no man can control.

Not nearly so drastic, but emphatic enough, is Godfrey Davies writing on *The Early Stuarts*, 1603–60. Of the husbandman of that time he says: 'He usually had a modest holding with rights of grazing on the common. He lived an arduous life in which all the family shared. Nevertheless independence and sufficiency seem to have been regarded as adequate reward for so much toil. . . . Generally the husbandmen found it necessary to work for wages, at harvest time, to secure ready money and purchase what was not produced on the little farm. The women and children of the family in addition to the help they gave out of doors, were busy indoors spinning thread which a weaver might make into cloth for their own use, or for sale to a clothier.' But for his food the husbandman, and indeed the yeoman and landowner of a grander sort, as well as the labourer, depended very largely indeed

25

on local products. How fallible this dependence was is shown by the issue of a small book by Sir Hugh Plat in 1596 under the title of *Sundrie new and Artificiall remedies against Famine: written* . . . *uppon thoccasion of this present Dearth:* but perhaps too much play has been made by some authorities with the suggestions put before an illiterate and unheeding public by Plat. It is undeniable that there were many seasons of dearth towards the end of Elizabeth's reign and in those of James I and Charles I, but such occasions were no more uncommon than the recurrent outbreaks of plague, and everyone who needed to be must have been well aware of the substitutes that could be employed to ward off actual starvation. More, the average man was thoroughly used to bread made of mixed grains and although he may have been unwilling for his bread to be further diluted, he preferred, unless he was a verv inhuman species, diluted bread to no bread at all.

Harrison is quite unequivocal on this subject. 'The bread throughout the land is made of such graine as the soile yieldeth, neverthelesse the gentilitie commonlie provide themselves sufficientlie of wheate.' The household and poor in some shires ate rye or barley and in times of scarcity 'beanes peason or otes' or all mixed and acorns added. The poor, of which class all the cottagers were, could not afford white wheaten bread. They ate what Harrison calls horse-corn, beans, peas, tares, oats and lentils, and this was true of all the champaign counties where the open field husbandry prevailed, and where 'much rie and barlie bread' was eaten, especially where 'wheat is scant and geson'. Fynes Moryson thought that English husbandmen preferred barley and rye bread 'as abiding longer in the stomach', and habit may have made these breads preferable. The idea that a diluted bread was more staying to the appetite continued to be held for at least two hundred years.

Nevertheless, with some show of reason, Harrison states, 'the English eat all they can buy' and comments despairingly on another change of habit, which he condemns by implication, but which was by no means so marked as it seemed to him . . . 'white meats, milke, butter and cheese, which were [never so dear as in my time, and] woont to be accounted of as one of the chief staies throughout the iland, are now reputed as food appurtinent onlie to the inferior sort, whilst such as are most wealthie doo feed upon the flesh of all kinds of cattel accustomed to be eaten, all sorts of fish taken upon our coasts, and in our fresh rivers, and such diversitie of wild and tame foules as are either bred in our iland or brought over unto us from other countries of the maine.' Drummond (*The Englishman's Food*) takes this to mean that the poor country people had in a degree given up the consumption of white meats in favour of flesh, but this is hardly borne out by the evidence of later times, although a further passage by Harrison lends some colour to the idea; in that passage Harrison is dealing more particularly with the artificer who lived near a well-provided meat market. He adds, however, that the husbandman 'wanteth it not at home, by his owne provision, which is at the best hand and commonlie least charge'. In spite of his list of foods, including all kinds of meat, he had no great opinion of the diet of the ordinary lower classes, some of whom got drunk and babbled at the numerous feasts because of the sparsity of the normal regimen. His words are: 'It may be that divers of them living at home, with hard and pinching diet, small drinke, and some of them having scarse enough of that, are soonest overtaken when they come to such bankets'.

The evidence of Harrison regarding the general character of the diet of the ordinary countrymen may be supplemented by two modern authorities. Lord Ernle writing in *Shakespeare's England* states that except in a salted state little meat was eaten. The medieval custom of fish twice a week was continued by Elizabeth. Veal and bacon was eaten at Easter and grass beef and peas on the feast of John the Baptist (24th June). There were, of course, many other feasts on which specially good food was eaten. G. M. Trevelyan in *England under the Stuarts* is more elaborate. 'The food of the farmhouse,' he says, 'which the unmarried "servant in husbandry" shared, varied according to each season of the year, with its traditional fasts and feasts. In Lent all ate fish— fresh if near seas and rivers, but salted if in dry or upland districts. . . . But the chief reason why the Lenten fast was still observed was because the ordinary rural household had no meat to hand at that time of the year except the flitch of bacon and the beef that had been slaughtered and salted last Martinmas day (11 November). At midsummer fresh beef and mutton was slaughtered amid general rejoicing, and continued to grace the table, until Winter . . . wild game could be killed by yeomen. . . . The farm which had to supply all the food of its inmates except perhaps a little bad food during Lent, could boast of a few vegetables in the garden but none in the fields. Fruit was more common; strawberries, raspberries and gooseberries had been grown in farm gardens fifty years before James came to the throne.'

Both these conclusions are based on one contemporary book, the well-known *Five hundred points of good husbandry* of Thomas Tusser, the first edition of which under the title of *One hundred points* appeared in 1557. Easter veal and bacon, for instance, are celebrated by this writer in the quatrain:—

> When Easter comes, who knows not than,
> that Veale and Baken is the man.
> And Martilmas beefe, doth beare good tacke:
> when countrie folk doe dainties lack.

Other verses provide the information given above, but none of this supplies any idea of the quantities eaten by the individual of any of the constituents of the diet indicated as normal. It is easy to conceive an exaggerated impression of the opulence of the feeding of the ordinary husbandman and labourer. Over a hundred years later the Revd. Richard Baxter's *Poor husbandman's advocate to rich racking landlords* was issued in 1691. Baxter did not pity the poor husbandman because his work was hard and he lived on coarse fare 'so they have but fire and cloathing to keepe them warme, and food that is not an enemy to health. For by the advantage of their labour and health, their browne bread and milk and butter and cheese and cabbages and turnips and parsnips and carrots and onions and potatoes and whey and buttermilk and pease pies and apple pies and puddings and pancakes and gruel and flummery and furmety, yea, dry bread and small drinke do afford their appetites a pleasanter relish . . . .'

Baxter thought farm servants were better off by the certainty of their condition and the landlord's servants actually better off because 'they feed on the variety of flesh and fish that cometh from their master's tables, when the poore tenants are glad of a piece of hanged bacon once a week, and some few that can kill a bull eate now and then a bit of hang'd biefe, enough to trie the stomach of an ostrige. He is a rich man that can afford to eate a jointe of fresh meate (biefe, mutton or veale) once in a month or fortnight. If their sow pigge or their hennes breed Chickens, they cannot afford to eate them, but must sell them to make their rent. They cannot afford to eate the egges that their hennes lay, nor the apples nor peares that grow on their trees (save some that are not vendible) but must make money of all. All the best of their butter and cheese they must sell, and feed themselves and children and servants with skimd cheese and skimd milke and whey curds. And through God's mercy all this doth them no harm'.

There is nothing here to justify any impression of a very ample meat diet; quite the contrary in fact, and the emphasis which has been laid upon the advantages the countryman got from a varied supply of home grown produce seems exaggerated. Baxter suggests the best of the produce had to be sold and the poorer quality eaten by the producer and this is only what might be expected. There is a contemporary saw which says that producers should 'Sell wheat and buy rye, Say the bells of Tenbury', as a good habit for an economical man with his way to make in the world. So far as meat itself is concerned the poor husbandman was not only unable to get it because of its monetary value, but the farming technique of the time was not sufficiently advanced to enable a supply of meat to be produced for the daily use of all the possible consumers. Enough meat was not only a dear commodity; it just did not exist.

Tusser mentions the advantages of a fish supplement to eke out the supplies of meat, fresh or dried and salted, according to the season of the year. He lived in and was acquainted with East Anglia and Essex, where the proximity of the sea-coast and the numerous rivers made a supply of fresh fish possible even in those days. The salt fish bought for winter supply and preserved by storing in a nest of peas haulm must have been an unappetising product when freshly obtained, but when it had been in store for a few months, with the inadequate methods of preserving then employed, it must have been appalling to a palate in any way dainty, if such a palate existed. The Yarmouth red herring was possibly the best of this sort of sea food. It was praised by John Taylor, the Water Poet, in 1622.

Actual examples of the composition of the daily meals are far to seek and the amount of each constituent used for each person still more so: but there is a contemporary account of the daily dietary of a schoolboy in a London school. This does not, like so many of the descriptions of Court and City feasts—the only real descriptions of meals that have come down to us and obviously quite exceptional—contain any exotic luxuries like peacock's tongues and may approximate, if reduced appropriately, to the daily regimen of the poor husbandman. 'Our breakfast in the morning,' says the boy, 'is, a little piece of bread not bulted, but with all the bran in it, and a little butter, or some fruite, according to the season of the yeare. To dinner we have herbes, or everyone a messe of porridge. Sometimes turneppes, coleworts, wheat and barley in porridge, a kind of delicat meate made of fine wheat flower and eggs. Upon fishe dayes, fleeted milke, in deepe porrengers (whereout the butter is taken) with some bread put in it. Some fresh fishe, if in Fish Streete it can be had at a reasonable price. If not, salt fishe, well wattered. After pease, or fitches, or beanes, or lupins. . . .' They drank small beer, or occasionally a little watered wine, and ate a little bread, or almonds, dried figs or raisins, or in summer a little fresh fruit as dessert. For supper salad, probably cabbage, lettuce, spinach and beetroots with salt, olive oil and vinegar. Stewed mutton with dried prunes, small roots or chopped herbs, 'a good gallimalfry' or minced meat. Some days they had roste meat, veal or kid, and on fasting days eggs, fried, poached or roasted, or in pancake, fish, cheese and nuts. Some considerable deductions would have to be made from this dietary to make it that of the cottager; especially as regards the daily supply of meat at the evening meal and the imported luxuries in the way of dried fruits and olive oil: but it is at least some indication of the make-up of the daily meal schedule of ordinary people.

There is one sentence that needs a little elaboration, the very first, 'a little piece of bread, not bulted, but all the bran in it'. This may have been a wholemeal wheat loaf, or it may have been a loaf made of the flour of mixed grains. As the place was London it is more likely to have been the former although even in London a meslin loaf, of mixed wheat and rye, was eaten, and as Harrison says, in bad times all sorts of admixtures were used.

In the country the admixtures were the ordinary routine and were commonplace of daily life. Henry Best,[1] lord of the manor of Elmswell in the East Riding has left a record of the corn he sent to the mill for use at home in 1641. 'Wee sende (in winter time) a mette (2 bushel) of massledine (mixed wheat and rye) for our own tempsed bread making; in the heate of summer wee sende but a bushell. . . .' The smaller quantity in the summer was because the bread would not keep so long. 'Wee sende for the brown bread (in winter time) a bushell of rye, a bushell of pease and a bushell of barley'; the grain was blended before it was sent to the mill. '. . . in summer time we send but a mette . . . viz. a bushell of peas and a bushell of rye, into which wee putt a ryinge or two or three of barley. Wee sende for our own pyes a bushell of the best wheate. We send for the folkes puddinges a bushell of barley' (never rye) . . . 'in harvest time they have wheat puddinges. The folkes pye crusts are made of massledine, as our bread is. . . . Poore folkes putt usually a pecke of pease to a bushell of rye; and some againe two peckes of pease to a frundell (2 pks.) of massledine and say that these make hearty bread. In many places they grinde after logginges of wheat for their servants pyes; and fewe there are that grinde any

---

[1] See *Farming and Account Books* in *Trans. Surtees Soc.* (1857), xxxiii.

barley att all for their household use because it is soe shorte and will not abide workinge.'

This, of course, only applies to the district concerned but barley bread must have been eaten in wide districts of the countryside, and the use of pease and other things as diluents was more than probably quite customary. W. H. Hudson[1] met a Wiltshire shepherd who had eaten barley bread as a usual thing two hundred years after Best wrote, and it has been remarked in other parts of the south and south-west. Joseph Arch,[2] the founder of the first really successful trade union of farm labourers in 1870, relates how in his childhood his mother wept because his father was out of work and the family was reduced to barley flour for the preparation of the home baked loaf. A food that was not unusual because of necessity in the nineteenth century was, we may be quite certain, quite as usual from necessity two centuries before. W. J. Ashley went to the trouble of writing a whole book, *The bread of our forefathers*, to show that rye was generally used, and was probably more usual in earlier times than wheat; he might have gone farther and pointed out that barley was consumed as bread as well as drunk as beer in many districts and that diluents like peas, beans, vetches and lupines were, to put it at a low level, not unknown.

Across the county from Elmswell, on the borders of Shropshire and Montgomery, lived the old, very old man, Thomas Parr, whose great age, well over a century, was celebrated in one of John Taylor's poems in 1635. Thomas Parr had not moved with the times 'And from his Father's function hath not gone'. For food

> *He was of old* Pythagoras *opinion*
> *That green cheese was most wholesome (with an onion)*
> *Course Meslin bread: and for his daily swig,*
> *Milk, Butter-Milk and Water, Whey and Whig;*
> *Sometimes Metheglin, and by fortune happy,*
> *He sometimes sipp'd a Cup of Ale most nappy,*
> *Cider or Perry when he did repair*
> *T'a Whitsun Ale, Wake, Wedding or a Fair,*
> *Or when at Christmas time he was a Guest,*
> *At his good Land-lords house amongst the rest . . .*
> *His physic was good butter which the soil of Salop yields*
> *. . . more sweet than* Candy oil.

[1] W. H. Hudson, *A Shepherd's Life* (1926 ed.), pp. 147–8.
[2] Joseph Arch, *The Story of his Life told by Himself* (1898).

Doubtless this information was vouchsafed in answer to the usual journalistic question put by Taylor 'To what do you attribute your great age?' and for that reason may be accounted accurate.

Some hundred miles south-east of old Parr's cottage there were folk songs which probably dated from the seventeenth century known to the local countrymen in our own days. These were collected by Alfred Williams[1] and a couple of them state the husbandman's feeding ideas. In the first of them, 'Old Moll', a lover asks his maid,

> *Wont some good fat bacon serve thy turn*
> *Some delicate powdered beef*
> *Some bread and cheese and milk, sweet Moll?*
> *That's farmer's food indeed . . . .*
>
> *Wont one good garment serve thy turn*
> *And petticoats likewise;*
> *Thy stockings of a good true blue,*
> *And thy shoes of the lowest price?*

The second, 'The husband and the servingman,' contains the husbandman's declaration,

> *As for your cock and capon*
> *Give me some beans and bacon*
> *And a pot of good ale now and then;*
> *For in a farmer's house*
> *There is good ham and souse*
> *That's your living for a husbandman.*

The south-western counties of Devon, Somerset and Cornwall were perhaps fortunate in being generally accessible to sea food, even in days of pack horse transport. J. Y. A. Mosshead, in *A History of Salcombe Regis*, seems to indicate that the tenant in that parish under James I, being out all day at work, only took two meals, a breakfast consisting of cheese from his own milk and cider from his own apples, presumably with bread, although that is not specifically stated, and an evening meal of salt pork and cider. There is a marked lack of precision in these statements, but they show that there was little difference in the diet of the tenantry of Salcombe Regis and elsewhere in the country. Richard Blackmore had a different idea of the larder of a well-to-do yeoman in Somerset under James II eighty years later. When Tom Faggus dropped

[1] Alfred Williams, *Folk Songs of the Upper Thames* (1923), pp. 95, 97 and 112.

IV WATTLE, DAUB AND THATCH COTTAGE
Manor Road, Didcot, Berks.

V A SIMILAR COTTAGE AT HAGBOURÑE, BERKSHIRE
Here, as above, the windows are probably of later date than the cottages

VI BRICK & THATCH
COTTAGE
with tiled gable at Hursley,
Hants, on the old Winchester
Road

VII COB COTTAGES
WIDECOMBE, DEVON, One is an Inn.   The windows are modern

in unexpectedly upon the Ridds at their farm near Exmoor, Mrs. Ridd is made to say 'Cousin Tom, we cannot entertain you as the lordly inns on the roads; and we have small change of victuals. . . . There are some few collops of red deer's flesh, and a ham just down from the chimney, and some dried salmon from Lynmouth weir, and cold roast pig, and some oysters'. It should be remarked that the majority of these things are natural produce, game and fish, to be had for the trouble of catching; the rest are pig—otherwise the feast is satisfying enough, especially when a little of each is taken as it was by Tom, but Mrs. Ridd wanted, like all housewives, to impress her visitor, and it is unlikely that all these things graced the board for one meal at ordinary times. Some of them could be got by most people either by legal prescription or in defiance of it.

In Cornwall there were specially famous local foods like saffron, pilchards and pasties filled with nothing in particular but everything in general. Carew's description, dated 1602, remarks that rye was only grown 'on those worst grounds, which will beare no wheate. Barley is growne into great use of late years . . . and in the deare seasons past the poore found happie benefit for they were principally relieved and the labourers also fed, by the bread made thereof. . . . In the Western part of Cornwall they carrie their Barley to the Mill within eight or nine weekes from the time that they sewed it; such an hastie ripening do the bordering Seas afford. This increase of Barley tillage, hath also amended the Cornish drinke, by converting that grain into Mault, which (to the il relishing of strangers) in former times they made onely of Otes'. Making malt of oats was not confined to Cornwall but was common in the Northern counties, where wormwood was used to give the drink length of life. The county was rich in wild and cultivated fruit. Whurts (blueberries), strawberries and raspberries were gathered for the taking, and pears, plums, cherries, mulberries, chestnuts and walnuts were grown in orchards. Furze and coppice wood was used as fuel, and some coal brought from Wales.

Mrs. Ridd referred to the luxurious living to be found at inns in 1680 odd; John Taylor, the Water Poet, who went on a walking tour from London to Edinburgh in 1618 which he called *The Pennyles Pilgrimage* waxed, as always, lyrical about it

> *I had good bacon, Neates-tongue, Cheese,*
> *With Roses, Barbaries, of each Conserves,*
> *And Mithridate, which vigorous health preserves.*

He travelled through Daventry, Lichfield, Newcastle-under-Lyme and north to Lancaster, finding,that he was given oats to eat at Manchester. Little wheat was grown in Lancashire at this time and the local regimen of this country and the north was limited to the so-called inferior grains, rye, oats and barley, and the bread was probably often made of mixed flour in much the same way as that of Henry Best on the other side of the Pennines.

Oats was, then, as in the early twentieth century, the chief grain grown in Cumberland, although in some districts barley was more general, and formed the staple food of the peasantry in the same forms of bread and malt as it did in Cornwall.

The Border in the reign of Elizabeth was necessarily strongly garrisoned and if D. W. Tough's[1] statements are correct the soldier's rations were extraordinarily generous, vast in quantity by any scale, modern or contemporary: but the theory may have been that he had a family to keep: otherwise the quantities given are stupendous. For what it is worth the statement is:

'Each day he (the soldier) had a twenty-four ounce loaf of wheaten bread at a 1d., a pottle of beer, apparently about two-thirds of a gallon, at a penny, two lb. of beef or mutton at 1¾d. a pound from Midsummer to January and 1½d. from January to Shrovetide, half a pound of butter and a pound of cheese. This extract from the victualler's contract for 1575 applied only to meat days. Eleven years later each man got bread, meat and beer as above, but nothing else on meat days, whereas on fish days the rations were bread and beer as above, with half a pound of butter or a pound of cheese, or a quarter of a "codd" or of "linge a reasonable pece", or seven or eight white herrings or red. In 1597 he got twelve ounces of bread, three pints of beer, ¾ lb. of cheese, and ¼ lb. of butter, or a pound and a half of beef instead of the last two. . . . In 1595 there were three fish days a week. The decrease in the ration was probably due to the increased price.' If any of these soldiers ever got such rations, it is reasonably certain that no cottager ever did, and if he did he died of a surfeit.

One innovation in food production did take place in the seventeenth century. It was the introduction of the potato, but there is no means of judging how widely it was grown nor how many people ate it. Sarah Fell, of Swarthmore Hall, Lancashire, bought setting potatoes between 1673 and 1678, but this is an isolated reference, although if

[1] D. W. Tough, *The Last Years of a Frontier: a History of the Borders during the Reign of Elizabeth* (1928), p. 46.

it was possible for her to buy them, it was possible for other people to do so, at all events to some degree. This is far from saying that they were extensively grown and eaten even in Lancashire, although there is reason to suppose that the tuber may have been better known in that county than elsewhere. It had a strong protagonist in John Forster, who wrote the first English book about it, under the title *England's Happiness Increased, or A Sure and Easie Remedy against all succeeding Dear Years; by a Plantation of the Roots called Potatoes* ... 1664; but writing a book about a new crop is a very different matter from getting people to grow it in their gardens or fields. Where it was adopted it certainly gave a little more assurance against the recurrent dearths of the time.

These dearths were sufficient to put an extreme edge on care, and little food was wasted, much being eaten in the way of preserved or semi-preserved meat that would to-day be condemned as unfit for consumption. The quantities eaten by the individual are difficult to arrive at; the schoolboy's regimen and the soldier's rations cited are not much help although they are indications, and as has been said, with suitable deductions the schoolboy's daily diet may have been something like what the cottager habitually ate. The soldier's rations are so generous as to be improbable even in those days of hearty trenchermen.

Normally the cottager's staples would be a bread of mixed flour, white meats, milk, buttermilk or whey and skim milk cheese, occasional meat meals, mainly derived from the pig, or at festivals beef, mutton and possibly poultry, for example, a Michaelmas goose, perhaps a wild rabbit. Home-made ale, and various home-made wines, cider the most usual, mead or metheglin, if bees were kept, and all sorts of concoctions made from flowers, berries and vegetables were the common drink. All these things taken together may have provided an ample table, particularly in good seasons, but the regimen was restricted to no more and no less than the local produce and its manipulation by the careful housewife. How far the cottage wife went in for making conserves, jam and general stillroom produce, like that which garnished the tables of great houses, it is not possible to say, but the diet, if not luxurious, was enough to sustain life by the mere fact that life continued, despite the recurrent incidence of plague, pestilence and famine.

PART TWO

GEORGIAN TIMES (1714–1837)

NOTABLE EVENTS

England was at war from some sixty-eight years, more than half the period from 1690 to 1815, but this did not much affect the common people while the country was still self-supporting. Jacobite Rebellions in 1715 and 1745. First newspaper, *Daily Courant*, 1702. Adam Smith's *Wealth of the Nations*, 1776.

Inventions and Improvements:
Hargreave's spinning jenny, 1764. Watt's steam-engine, 1765. Arkwright's spinning machine, 1768. Crompton's mule, 1776. Brindley's canals from 1767.

Agricultural pioneers and social reformers:
Agricultural: Jethro Tull (1674–1741). 'Turnip' Townsend (1674–1738). Robert Bakewell (1725–95). Coke of Norfolk. *Social reformers:* Arthur Young (1741–1820). William Cobbett (1762–1835). John Wesley (1703–91). John Howard (1726–90).

Population of England
1801, 9 million. 1821, 12 million.

IV INTRODUCTORY

THE turn of a century or the accession of a new reigning house has no cataclysmic effect upon the life of the rural classes; but these defined periods are a convenience. There was, of course, no drastic change in the general living conditions of the cottager between 1699 and 1700, nor when George I came to the throne a few years later. Certain tendencies which had been noticeable in the later years of the seventeenth century developed as the eighteenth century went on.

'Political arithmetic' was then what are now called 'vital statistics', but was only estimates and intelligent or unintelligent guesses. Increased interest in this subject led to discussions of the relative value to society as a whole of the different classes, and the 'labouring poor', who were regarded by the late seventeenth century writers as non-productive, became steadily more appreciated by the social philosophers as the eighteenth century advanced. Instead of being non-productive they came to be regarded as the foundation and prop of society, the people who produced all the wealth that others consumed. For the philosophers there was a gap between theory and practice. They could not understand why the labourer, who obviously deserved at least a minimum of comfort, did not always get it, and it grew increasingly clear with the passage of the years that the labourer and the peasant were not getting better off but worse. The yeoman, it has been said, was being steadily reduced to a peasant and the peasant to a wage-earner. This was certainly not everywhere true, because some of these people rose in status for one reason or another.

The main factor in the depression of the small men is usually accepted to have been the accelerated rate of enclosure of the open fields and wastes, a process which has been described so often that it need not be discussed again here. Its effects were plain enough. All authorities are agreed upon them, and, in addition, there was the definitely stated advice of a land steward to his employees given in the early seventeen-hundreds to buy up small freeholds and copyholds to round off the estate, a practice that all landowners great and small have indulged in in all ages in one way or another. It may be that the pre-enclosure age is painted in too halcyon colours. As we have seen, there was little comfort in it, but a harsh life is not necessarily an unhappy one, and there must have been opportunities on a limited scale in the older days that certainly ceased to exist in the newer.

For the cottager, wage earner and husbandman alike, these opportunities lay mainly in the possibility of stock farming on the wastes, either of prescriptive right or by tolerance, and it was only with the acceleration of the enclosure movement around 1760 that these rights were abolished in wider and wider districts. Before they vanished, the farm servant, who waited till he had accumulated a little savings for marriage, could invest in livestock of one sort or another when he set up house for himself, and put them on the wastes to keep themselves. The day labourer, if he was ever able to save, could do the same, and both, just as the small husbandman could, very likely grew a part of the family subsistence in a garden plot or on the minute holding in the common fields. Squatters on the common who had made small, possibly illegal, intakes, were in very much the same position. Such rights as these were rarely adequate to a complete living; they formed a basis on which a living could be made if supplemented by other activities, working for a wage at various jobs or the practice of a handicraft. Their loss destroyed a factor which made for independence; but long before there had been a vast problem of poverty from the days of the Tudors, and this problem was no less in the century 1660–1760 than it was before; it was certainly not so poignant as it became with the economic changes that took place in the following hundred years.

Since the days of Elizabeth the parish had been ordered to look after its own poor, by relief, setting to work and punishment where necessary; again and again legislators tried to find a remedy for this distress by Act of Parliament. The feeling that local poverty should be taken care of locally was finally codified in the Law of Settlement passed in 1662. The Act practically made society, so far as the labouring poor were society, static; the poor man became a prisoner in his own parish if he wished to qualify for parish relief when overtaken by misfortune: and each parish vied with the other in trying to get rid of the impotent poor, as they were called, so that they would become chargeable elsewhere, if they became chargeable at all.

Poor relief was, if Gregory King is to be believed, part of the regular livelihood of a proportion of the population that would have appalled our Government of the peace years between 1918 and 1939. An analysis of the situation as described by King in 1688 and accepted by his contemporaries has been made by Mrs. Dorothy George in *England in Transition*. 'More than half the population, [King] calculated, were "decreasing the wealth of the kingdom", that is their expenses exceeded their earnings, and the deficiency had to be made up from poor relief, charity or plunder. His calculations are based on "families" or households—at one end of the scale is the peer's "family" of forty persons, which would include all his indoor servants, not excepting his chaplain: at the other end is the vagrant with no family at all. The phrase "decreasing the wealth of the kingdom" is itself significant of the point of view, for though it may fairly be given to the vagrant, its application to the labouring man whose utmost efforts cannot support a wife and family at the rate of wages begs a great many questions.

'This submerged or "unprofitable" majority, dependent in varying degrees on the charity of the nation (2,795,000 out of a total of 5,500,500 persons) included whole classes, "labouring people and out-servants 364,000 families, averaging 3½ persons or 1,300,000 souls; 400,000 families (or 1,300,000 souls) of "cottagers and paupers", and 35,000 families of "common soldiers" making together 222,000 souls. These are the classes which the eighteenth century lumped together as "the labouring poor".' Vagrants to the number of 30,000 complete the total. By 1775 *The Universal Dictionary of Trade and Commerce* estimated that out of a population of six million, 2,947,917 were the total of the 'decreasing' class, an improved proportion.

In addition to these people whose incomes were always, or frequently, below the level of their cost of living, as it would be put to-day, there were some 150,000 families of small farmers whose lot was often harder than that of their employees because they had to undertake the hazards of business, 'struggling with the alternate evils of bad seasons and bad markets' and only just able to keep their heads above water with an estimated average income of £44 and expenses of £42 10s. These men were really cottagers, although the contemporary meaning of the word cottage was a small house or hovel with little or no land.

All this sounds very desperate, but it was possibly not so bad as it sounds. Hardship is the concomitant of all pioneer living, and England was still in the late seventeenth and eighteenth centuries in the pioneer stage of development. Wide areas of marsh, fen, forest and waste were brought into cultivation and given their modern appearance during the eighteenth century and first half of the nineteenth. Population was scanty, some 5½ million at the beginning, some ten million at the end of the eighteenth century. And when all are poor, or the majority are poor, there is an equality of conditions which is accepted, as poverty then was by rich and poor alike. Towards the end of the eighteenth century as prices rose, and particularly when they sky-rocketted during the French Wars from 1792 to 1815, the poverty of the poor, whose dependence had come to be almost wholly on their inadequate wages, grew more severe, and the wealth of farmer and landowner grew so much greater that a vast gap came to separate these classes. This has never since been bridged, in spite of the recurrent depressions of the nineteenth century, the first of which followed the wars and lasted intermittently until the accession of Victoria. It was remarked by Robert Bloomfield at the time,

> *Whene'er refinement shows its hated face:*
> *. . . 'tis the peasant's curse:*
> *That hourly makes his wretched station worse;*

by Elie Halévy in *A History of the English People in* 1815 (1924), and in more frivolous fashion by Wyndham Lewis in *Mysterious Mr. Bull.*

The hard and poverty-stricken life of the cottager, which had been accepted as inevitable, but worthy of charitable assistance in the late seventeenth and early eighteenth centuries, came to be a social problem by the end of the eighteenth century. The philosophic attitude that the 'labouring poor' were the source of wealth and the development of 'political arithmetic' into the beginnings of modern economics with the writings of Steuart and Adam Smith led to enquiries into the actual position of the cottager. From these a much more exact idea of the real condition of the people can be secured than is possible from earlier sources. The first and foremost of these are Davies, *Case of the Labourers in Husbandry* (1795), and Eden, *State of the Poor* (1797). It is fortunate that people were moved to carry out such investigations or there might have been no accurate knowledge of what conditions really were. The cottager in the vast majority of cases ceased in the eighteenth century to have goods of value enough to justify him in making a will, and consequently the number of inventories of his goods is reduced. There were some other occasions when lists were made, and a few of them have come down to us: thus it is possible to learn with a moderate degree of accuracy how the labourer lived under the House of Hanover.

V COTTAGES

Two important influences bore upon cottage building in Georgian times, one legislative, the other cultural. The first was the doubtless well intentioned but misguided Act of Settlement of 1662; the second was the development of the cult of the picturesque, both of which continued to exercise their influence until well into the reign of Queen Victoria.

The Act of 1662 which tied a man to the parish where he was born, in intention, if not wholly in effect, was designed by a government of landowners. They could not possibly have foreseen the necessity for permitting complete mobility to labour which was to arise a century later with the birth of modern industry. They were accustomed to think of the manor or the parish as an entity, perhaps controlled by one or more of their number, and depending on its farming for its living. They were also used to the paternalistic attitude which thought that any member of a family must be supported by the rest of the family if he fell upon evil times, and this in spite of their harshness in dealing with the problems of vagrancy and the undeserving poor. They therefore thought that if a man were born in a place he had rights and duties in that place: besides they wanted labour for their increasingly commercial farming. And they wanted to avoid an influx of paupers who must be supported out of the rates in addition to those possessing settlement in the place. To make the mixture of motives more complex, there had been among the Puritans a growing feeling that poverty must necessarily be the result of sin of some sort or other, it must be a deserved condition in fact.

The squirearchy were, of course, not at all blind to their own interests, and doubtless many of those who had come back to their estates in the train of Charles II, as well as those who reaped some reward for their services to the Prince of Orange some thirty years later, soon saw how to circumvent some of the intentions of the Act. If a man owned a whole parish, and some of the great landlords owned literally hundreds, it was possible to avoid some part of the incidence of the poor rate. Cottages could be left to decay and become uninhabitable even by the low standards of the day, or they could be pulled down, so that the cottagers were forced to find accommodation in a neighbouring parish, where the whole was not in one pair of hands, or where there was still unoccupied and unenclosed waste on which they could squat. Once this had been achieved the landowners and farmers of the parish had created what came to be known as a 'closed' parish where no poor's rates were levied because there were no poor. Near by in the adjacent 'open' parish the incidence of the Poor rate was high, and from there the cottagers had to walk to their work in the closed parish. This opposition of the closed and open parish continued till 1867.

The possibility of creating a closed parish in this way had some bearing on the development of the cult of the picturesque, for it made its expression in the realm of cottage building realizable. What this cult really amounted to was an attempt to make landscape look like a contemporary painting. Its rise and development have been carefully traced by Christopher Hussey in *The Picturesque*. Great landowners under the influence of Vanbrugh, at Castle Howard in Yorkshire, Claremont House at Esher, in Surrey, and elsewhere, had already been experimenting in this direction when Addison wrote in 1712: 'Why may not a whole estate be thrown into a kind of garden by frequent plantations? A man might make a pretty Landskip of his own possessions.' Anyone who undertook to do this would be driven to the obvious necessity of beautifying the farmhouses and the cottages in the village: and with these theories came a series of writers who 'explored every avenue of the subject' thoroughly. A select list of them will be found in the bibliography. In the text they will be referred to by name. Both these writers and the landowners who put their theories into practice were more interested with appearances than sanitary considerations; but the picturesque builders provided cottages, not without some very marked disadvantages to the people who lived in them, but a good deal better than contemporary builders provided in open villages. Examples given by Hussey are Blaise near Bath, which was the work of John Nash, the architect of old Regent Street. This is a village of thatched cottages surrounding a green on which a combined sundial and pump was erected. It was built in 1809 for J. S. Harford. William Mason was a landscape gardener: he was employed by Lord Harcourt to lay out his grounds at Nuneham Courtenay and the village was rebuilt at the same time. All the cottages are built of brick and timber to the same design and placed at intervals along both sides of the main Oxford–London road. Milton Abbas, Dorset, was probably rebuilt by Sir William Chambers about 1775, and is a delightful spot. There are many other examples and the cottages are still occupied. The disadvantages endured by the occupants were emphasized by Christopher Holdenby in 1913 when his book *The Folk of the Furrow* appeared. '. . . only too often are the inhabitants made to suffer for the artistic sloping roofs and tiny windows. When one has no choice of bedrooms, gables and eaves are often a picturesque cruelty by every inch of height and light and air of which they deprive human beings. . . . As every inch of space is reduced, these details become more insupportable—windows made never to open, or, in tiny rooms, occupying the only wall space where a bed can be placed.' Be that as it may, the picturesque cottage built in the eighteenth and early nineteenth century was a better place to live in than many of the hovels to be found outside the rigid bounds of the cult.

The contrast was made clear by some of the contemporary reformers. 'Humanity shudders,' says Thomas Davis,[1] Steward to the Marquis of Bath, in 1795, 'at the idea of the industrious labourer, with a wife and five or six children, being obliged to live or rather to exist, in a wretched, damp, gloomy room, of 10 or 12 ft. square, and that room without a floor; but common decency must revolt at considering, that over this wretched apartment, there is only *one* chamber, to hold all the miserable beds of the miserable family.' Similar language was used by Nathaniel Kent[2] twenty years earlier. 'The shattered hovels,' he says, 'which half the poor of this kingdom are obliged to put up with, is truly affecting to a heart fraught with humanity. Those who condescend to visit these miserable tenements can testify that neither health nor decency can be preserved in them.' There was thus ample reason for rebuilding in addition to the desire of the wealthy landowner to embellish his estate and to restrict the number of cottages upon it to

[1] Thomas Davis, *Address to the Landholders of this Kingdom; with Plans of Cottages* in *Letters and Communications to the Bath and West Soc.*(1795), vii, p. 295. —See also F. G. Heath, *The English Peasantry* (1874), p. 54.—William Howitt *The Rural Life of England* (1838), i, pp. 139 and 167.—William Crossing, *A Hundred Years of Dartmoor* (1902, 5th ed.), p. 78.

[2] Nathaniel Kent, *Hints to Gentlemen of Landed Property* (1775), p. 229. See similar notes in James M'Phail, *A Treatise on the Culture of the Cucumber* (1794), p. 359.

that which would house people he knew would not become chargeable to the Poor Rate.

Besides such cottagers as were regular tenants of village homes that were being improved and restricted in numbers for the dual reasons given, the development of the enclosure movement dispossessed the squatters who had secured no legal right to their hovels and intakes. The eviction of these squatters, where they were evicted, created a local housing problem. Indeed the housing of labourers as a whole was deteriorating by 1775, not so much in quality as in accommodation. The dispossessed often found themselves crowded into old farmhouses in the 'open' village or having to share the larger cottages between two or more families.

The condition of the squatters as such varied as much as the conditions of any particular class of people varies. Arthur Young, the great protagonist of improved farming of the day, described a village of squatters who had reclaimed some 40 acres of the 700 acres of heath at Blofield in Norfolk. The lord of the manor had not stopped building here in 1801, and there were thirty families in the village in good cottages, some worth £40 to £60. In Salop on the contrary, Bishton, the reporter on the county, thinks the cottages and fields of squatters were extremely miserable. The squatters had a sort of independence but worked for day wages as well. It was the repeal of the Act of 1589 (the 4a Act) in 1775 that made the process of absorbing these plots legal, in addition, of course, to the local Enclosure Act when it was obtained.

And there was another factor which most writers have not discussed when approaching rural housing conditions in the eighteenth century. The population was increasing slowly in the first half of the century, more rapidly in the second half and more rapidly still in the first half of the nineteenth century. Many of the increase in the nineteenth century were housed in the new industrial towns, but a population which rose from about 5½ million in 1700 to nearly ten million in 1800 must have caused some congestion in the villages, especially under the conditions laid down by the Act of Settlement. There was thus every reason for cottage building at that time, and already by 1750 architects were interesting themselves in the design of farmhouses: those who made designs for, or wrote about, the plan of cottages were in the main reformers.

Even so famous an architect as Sir John Soane[1] was moved to write

---

[1] Sir John Soane, *Sketches in Architecture* (1793).

about cottages and villas. His book on houses having been favourably received he was 'induced to offer another publication ... consisting of cottages for the laborious and industrious part of the community'. This enthusiasm, primarily a matter of fashion, may have been partly a matter of realizing that cottages were not invariably all they should be.

John Wood, the architect of Bath,[1] who was certainly super-conscientious, thought he ought to see cottages before producing his designs. 'The greater part of the cottages that fell within my observations,' he says, 'I found to be shattered, dirty, inconvenient, miserable hovels, scarcely affording a shelter for the beasts of the forest, much less were they proper habitations for the human species.' He was particularly emphatic on the necessity for a privy to each, an ideal not realized for a hundred years after he expressed it, 'many of our village streets being only a "jake" '. Crabbe[2] describes such a village street:

> Between the road way and the walls, offense,
> Invades all eyes and strikes on every sense;
> There lie, obscene, at every open door,
> Heaps from the hearth and sweepings from the floor,
> And day by day the mingled masses grow,
> As sinks are disembogued and kennels flow.
> There hungry dogs and hungry children steal
> There pigs and chickens quarrel for a meal.

Other reformers of the later years of the eighteenth century were impressed with the necessity for better housing for the 'useful and truly valuable description of persons, the labourers who are employed in husbandry', but they were not prepared to go too far.

The suggestions of Nathaniel Kent were humanitarian, and were adopted by Lord Brownlow and other landowners occupied with agricultural improvements, but in spite of his condemnation of existing cottages, Kent did not invite too great expense for his patrons. He acknowledges, like so many eighteenth century and earlier writers, that 'cottagers are indisputably the most beneficial race of people we have'. Yet he was 'far from wishing to see the cottage improved or augmented so as to make it fine and expensive. ... All that is requisite is a warm, comfortable, plain room for the poor inhabitants to eat their morsel in, an oven to bake their bread, a little receptacle for their small beer and provisions and two wholesome lodging apartments, one for the man

[1] John Wood, *A Series of Plans for Cottages* (new ed., 1792), p. 2.
[2] Rev. George Crabbe, *The Village* (1783).

and his wife and another for his children. It would perhaps be more decent if the boys and girls could be separated, but this would make the building too expensive (*sic*) and besides is not so materially necessary; for the boys find employment in farmhouses at an early age'. He supplies plans and specifications. His cottages might, if the estate could provide timber, be built of wood, or, if not, of brick and tile. He recommended that each should have half an acre of land attached to it, at the same rent per acre as the farmer paid.

The specification calls for walls 14 in. thick (of brick) to the chamber floor and 9 in. above; the lower rooms to be 7 ft. high in the clear. The smallest was to have a living room 12½ ft. square, a pantry 6 ft. by 4½ ft., a cellar 7½ ft. by 6 ft. and two bedrooms of 12½ ft. by 11 ft. and 12½ ft. by 7½ ft. This was certainly not excessive and the cost, built of brick, was estimated at £66; of wood only £58. The proposed rent was 5 per cent.

Thomas Davis was a trifle more benevolent and explicit. The lower rooms should be at least 7 ft. high under the beams, the upper at least 6 ft. 8 in. Cottages should be built of the rough stone of the neighbourhood, and with elm or fir timber, roofed with thatch. The ground floor was to be paved with stone or brick, all the rooms to be plastered, and all the upper rooms to be ceiled. The smallest cottage was to have three rooms below and two above, with a skilling behind for fuel, and was estimated to cost £50.

Beatson[1] is a little conservative in the ideas he submitted to the Board of Agriculture in 1797. His plans of cottages have one, two or three rooms; more he evidently considers excessive. 'Those of four,' he says, 'are seldom built, and are more in the style of houses of a superior kind. Henry Holland, the fashionable architect of Carlton House, in the same year proposed a living room 12 ft. square and 8 ft. high and a small room to be used as a cellar, dairy or for other purposes, with two bedrooms above. His opinion is shared by Mr. Crutchley.[2]

Even greater refinements were suggested only four years later by the author of *The Modern Land Steward* (1801). The floor should be 16 in. or 18 in. above the ground, clear of banks. Rooms not less than 8 ft. high, no chambers in the roof; walls, if stone 16 in. thick, if brick, a brick and a half. A porch or shed to screen the entrance from the rain or wind and to contain tools should be added. There should be

[1] Robert Beatson, *On Farm Buildings in General in Communications to the Board of Agric.* (1797), i, p. 296.
[2] Mr. Crutchley, *On Cottages* in ibid., p. 103.

a privy; the stairs should be not less than 3 ft. wide with a tread not less than 9 in. In addition to these careful demands there should be one lodging room for the parents, another for the female, a third for the male children; moreover the cottages should be built in pairs, and, greatest refinement of all, ought to be built in the vicinity of water.

This writer is a disciple of Wood, whose plans are for cottages of one to four rooms, and Wood's accommodation is more than endorsed by Sir John Soane. Other writers who believe in ample accommodation —they afford two rooms down and at least two upstairs—are John Plaw[1] and D. Laing.[2] But Plaw's cottages are expensive in cost, and as he was more interested in cottages that could be described as shooting lodges,[3] it may be that he was too ideal. He does state the materials of his proposed structures, and they are commonplace; pisé, clay, rubblestone and brick panelling, the latter lime washed and the former rough cast or plastered, thatched roofs and brick paved floors in the living rooms are the simplicity he specified.

These generous plans are in contrast to those proposed by J. Miller.[4] His smallest cottages are one storey and have only a living room 15 ft. by 11 ft., a bedroom 9 ft. by 7 ft. and a closet. His two-storey plans are not clear. They may be cottages of one room below and one room above or more.

He is not capable of Wood's refinements; his raised floor was certainly something new: most of the specifications call for stone, or brick or tiled floors, and these were presumably laid upon the earth. So late as 1761 John Mordant, author of *The Compleat Steward*, was content with earth floors for 'little cottages'. These floors were made of one-third lime, one-third coal ashes well sifted and one-third loamy clay and horse dung made from grass, these two last in equal proportions; *if either is wanting of its proportion let it be the ashes*. Another sort might be made of loamy clay with one-third new soft horse dung made from grass with a small quantity of coal ashes. The material was tempered, rested for ten days, again tempered and rested for three days, thereafter being laid upon the ground. This description is copied almost verbally from the *Dictionarium Rusticum*, first issued in 1704, and under the name of lime-ash floors was a well-established practice.

[1] John Plaw, *Sketches of Country Houses* (1800).
[2] D. Laing, *Hints for Dwellings* (1800).
[3] John Plaw, *Rural Architecture* (1794).
[4] J. Miller, *The Country Gentlemen's Architect* (1787), Plates i and ii.

E

Even in 1831 cottages of clay and straw walls and pole and thatch roofs with one living room 14 ft. by 13 ft. and two bedrooms 10 ft. by 9 ft. 2 in. on the ground floor and a loft above were proposed by Thomas Postans.

So far the plans detailed are only for proposed cottages. They had evidently received some thought, and may be somewhat in advance of the current practice, as they commonly are, but this was not likely to be very marked.

A careful analysis of the evidence of the county reports, prepared in two or more editions, each for the old Board of Agriculture, between 1794 and 1815, about the actual housing of the rural population at the end of the eighteenth century, made by Sir John Clapham, is given here in brief and the evidence is examined in detail later. His statement of the conditions is quite accurate,[1] and is confirmed by Sir Frederick Eden in his great work on *The State of the Poor*, 1797.

Broadly, the houses of Britain grew steadily worse to the northward, reaching the lowest average level in Scotland and Wales; but very ugly corners were found almost everywhere. The typical cottage south of the Thames, for example, was a fairly substantial structure, brick built or half timbered, with glazed windows, and in some districts covered with a vine. It might have but a single bedroom, for in no part of the country was even the three-room cottage universal, and in places the cottages were of the one bedroom, 'hay-loft' type; but it could at least be called a house. Yet there were plenty of Dorset cottages with mud walls made of road scrapings in 1794, and on the outskirts of the wastes in Surrey and Hants, in the 'twenties were still to be found the turf huts of squatters—so long as the farmers tolerated them.

In an elaboration of these remarks, too extensive to be fully quoted, Clapham points out that though mud cottages were found scattered up and down in most parts of the country, and were typical in some of the more remote districts, yet the most usual dwelling was of stone, brick or half-timber, with one or two rooms upstairs, and some glazed, if unopened, windows. Thatch or tile was the usual roof, or sometimes local stone or slate slabs. There was not much to choose between the better cottages and the smaller farmhouses. Such comfortable houses as there were, and they were increasing, although not necessarily

---

[1] Sir John Clapham, *Economic History of Modern Britain in the Railway Age: 1820–50* (1926), p. 27 *et seq.* See also G. F. Innocent, *The Development of English Building Construction* (1916), p. 36. For Wales see Evan J. Jones, *Some Contributions to the Economic History of Wales* (1928), pp. 21–2.

occupied by farmer or labourer, were mainly not more than fifty, although a few were a hundred years, old.

This excellent description of housing conditions at the end of the century is not very different from one that could be drawn of the beginning. The main thing is that some improvements had certainly been made, the earlier period requiring heavier shading in the dark parts and less light in the districts which had been improved in the 'improving' century.

In the Home Counties, which were the best housed at the end of the century, it is probable that the more regular intercourse of a larger proportion of the population with London influenced the builders to use the most modern practice of all times; but Wm. Ellis in *Chiltern and Vale Farming Explained*, somewhat pityingly, says that, in Hertfordshire in 1733 'red clay . . . by being beat and tempered with short cut straw, often supplies the place of Boards to the sides of a poor man's cottage, with the help of Hazel or other Poles'. He did not apparently envisage the extravagance of brick for a poor man's cottage. Most of the houses in the district were of brick, but brick and stud walls and straw thatch were not uncommon between Woodford, Essex, and Little Gaddesden, Herts., in 1748 when Pehr Kalm,[1] a touring Swede, visited the district. In houses of two or three storeys here, the upper were often 'of thin boards and laths, daubed on the outside as well as the inside with clay and lime, so that it seems as though they were of stone'. The upper floors were of imported deal and the lower of tile or stone. Such a construction may be favourably compared with the flimsy suburban buildings remarked as increasing rapidly between London and Hertfordshire in 1810 by L. Simond,[2] another tourist, this time a Frenchman. For ten miles out of London 'you travel between two rows of brick houses . . . their walls are frightfully thin, a single brick of 8 in.—and instead of beams, mere planks lying on an edge'.

In the neighbouring county of Buckingham the older houses were poor, but the new were improved, being built of brick and thatch or mud and timber quarterings with thatched roofs. The houses in the open field parishes were reported bad in 1794,[3] while nine years later

[1] Pehr Kalm, *Kalm's Account of his Visit to England on his Way to America in 1748* (1892), Tr. by Joseph Lucas, pp. 181-2, 201.

[2] L. Simond, *Journal of a Tour and Residence in Great Britain by a French Traveller* (1815), ii, p. 199.

[3] William James and James Malcolm, *General View . . . Agriculture of Bucks,* (1794), p. 11

the cottages were as good (the word should perhaps be bad) as are to be found in other counties.[1] In 1797 a tourist, Henry Wigstead, remarks that Stony Stratford is built of stone or brick.[2]

Essex was more fortunate. Colchester, of more importance then than now, was mostly of brick, wood and plaster, treated ornamentally, in the early years of the century according to M. Misson, another French tourist whose *Memoirs* appeared in 1719.[3] The farmhouses were of brick and timber with tiled roofs, and were two or three storeys high, although outhouses were sometimes of weather-board or furze walls; barns were sometimes built of brick and thatched, while some cottages were built of weather-board and thatch, reed thatch being used near the Thames; but those farmers who had thatch roofs were replacing them with tiles, as they could afford it when Kalm saw them in 1748. Nevertheless Young reported in 1807 that many of the small farms in the county were little better than cottages; others of larger size were formerly mansions. The then modern cottages were of brick and tile, those of lath and plaster being of a superior style; the old were generally of clay daubing in bad repair and imperfectly thatched.[4] Harwich, though not a big town, was an important port of transit to the Continent, but still consisted partly of wooden houses in 1762 when Count Frederick Kilmansegge landed there.[5]

Norfolk and Suffolk, counties where greatly improved farming had been introduced, were only fortunate in their buildings where the great improvers had been at work. Walpole, in the early part of the century, made Houghton a neat village of brick buildings, uniform within and without, for his own appropriate little tenantry with rents at a guinea a year. Forty or fifty families were housed here in 1799, and the rent was only charged at a shilling instead of a guinea, if S. J. Pratt[6] can be believed. Coke later in the century had built improved cottages at Holkham. These were in groups of four, backing on to one another, and had a living room 14 ft. by 14 ft., a room in one storey at

[1] Rev. St. John Priest, ibid. (1813), p. 46.

[2] Henry Wigstead, *Remarks on a Tour through N. and S. Wales in the Year* 1797, p. 4.

[3] M. Misson, *Memoirs and Observations in his Travels over England* (1719). Tr. by Mr. Ozell.

[4] Arthur Young, *General View . . . Agric. of Essex* (1807), pp. 45, 49.

[5] County Frederick Kilmansegge, *Diary of a Journey to England in* 1761-2 (1902). Tr. by Countess Kilmansegge, p. 16.

[6] S. J. Pratt, *Gleanings in England* (1799), i, p. 261.

the end of the block 11 ft. by 7 ft. 6 in. and a coal house, with possibly only one bedroom above. The frontispiece to the *Annals of Agriculture* for 1793 showing them is not too explicit. In 1781 Ipswich was condemned by Mrs. Philip Lybbe Powys for its 'dreadful narrow streets, poor looking old houses, and altogether a most melancholy place'.

Simond,[1] a more optimistic observer, reports in 1810 that in these two counties large farmhouses are seen with all their outbuildings substantial and complete, but so few cottages that he was unable to discern where or how the common labourers lived. In Suffolk he did see a few villages where the cottages were poor enough on the outside, but the casements in good repair, and, a tribute to the industry of the housewives, the floors clean. The large farmhouses are attributed in the *Annals* for 1784 to the prevalence of substantial owner occupiers, who had built good brick houses before then, with enclosed and well-managed gardens and had erected many new cottages, e.g. at Alderton.

The improved cottage in this district was very limited in its accommodation. Young[2] thinks it worthy of remark that two cottages with flint walls 18 in. thick, a living room 15 ft. by 11 ft. and a wood-room and a bedroom in a lean-to on the ground, both very small, and a bedchamber over each, had been built, and that near Dereham a new cottage contained a living room 12 ft. square, a lean-to and one bedchamber. Of Suffolk he gives no real details, but although the farmhouses had been much improved in the preceding twenty years, too often they were built of lath and plaster in 1797, and the cottages were then 'in general bad habitations, deficient in all contrivance for warmth or for convenience . . . in bad repair'.

Kent was better off than Suffolk. Kalm does not record his impressions of the farmhouses and cottages here as he does in Hertfordshire: he notices, however, that when he was coming up the Thames the houses (he does not say on which bank) were beautiful and mostly of brick, yet he saw some small buildings of crossbeams covered with boards. He also comments that Deal was almost entirely built of brick and tile. Near Maidstone, some fifty years later, William Marshall[3] describes the houses as still being chiefly of wood or half timber, with panels sometimes of plaster or brick. Studwork faced with flat tiles, scalewise, was also present, but most modern houses were brick built and tiled.

Surrey and Sussex are not described very fully by travellers, but the

[1] L. Simond, *op. cit.*, i, pp. 181, 189.

[2] Arthur Young, *General View . . . Agric. of Suffolk* (1797), pp. 10–11.

[3] William Marshall, *Rural Economy of the Southern Counties* (1798), i, pp. 30–1.

county reporters[1] say that the houses in Surrey were old and dilapidated, especially in the Vale or Weald, although in other parts large and in good repair. The older buildings were of brick and heavy slatestone, others of brick nogging, covered with tiles. Many were, however, of wood, lathed and plastered, or roughcast. The cottages are equivocally said to be sufficiently large and convenient for the people who occupy them. Sussex had the advantage of quarries and near them stone was used for building, while flint was used on the Downs, the cottages being constructed of the same local materials. Tiles were much used as a facing for houses in this county. Marshall,[2] however, remarks upon the timber and weather-board houses in the Weald, where they were roofed with thatch, tiles or chips.

Travelling south-westward the cottage accommodation grew steadily worse in Hampshire, Berkshire, Wiltshire and Dorset, particularly where the farms were large. On the chalk hills of Hampshire and Wiltshire, Marshall says that the larger farms were of brick and tile, the smaller of 'cob' and thatch, the size of holdings being extremely various. Earth walls were common in Wiltshire, but the houses had brick foundations and corners. Between Stourhead and Sherborne sandstone walls prevailed, and were commended in the *Annals* (1796) as making the houses dry.

In Berkshire[3] where the farms were generally large and the farmhouses and buildings good, built of brick or stone with tile or slate roofs, the cottages were very bad, having broken windows, ragged thatch, earth floors and frequently only one bedchamber, and in those districts of Wiltshire where consolidation had taken place, the surplus houses were let to labourers, to how many families is not stated, but more than one is certain, and the buildings were allowed to fall into decay.[4] The west or chalky part of Hampshire was better supplied with cottages than most parts, probably on account of the very general use of cob walls, a material which becomes steadily more common as progress westwards is made. At the end of the century many of the larger farms in this county occupied the smaller granges or manor houses of former times, but the farmhouses themselves were mostly

---

[1] William James and James Malcolm, *op. cit.*, p. 60.—William Stevenson, *General View . . . Agric. of Sussex* (1809), pp. 79, 83.

[2] William Marshall, *op. cit.*, ii, pp. 314, 319.

[3] William Pearce, *General View . . . Agric. of Berks.* (1794), p. 9.—William Mavor, ibid. (1808), pp. 62, 67, 72.

[4] Thomas Davis, *General View . . . Agric. of Wilts.* (1813), p. 9.

very ancient. For the new, all the available building materials were used, stone, flint, brick, cob or mud and various timbers. One Mr. Brimstone made an innovation here. He built cottages of brick, for two, three or four families with a common room, having a kitchen, etc. When he built single cottages he provided a living room 10 ft. by 15 ft. with a brick floor, in spite of the general prevalence of the cob cottage.[1]

Probably cob was the material used for building by the squatters in the New Forest who, the Rev. William Gilpin complains in 1781, 'build their little huts and inclose their little gardens and patches of ground without leave'. He tells the old story of houses being built in a single night, the small possessions moved in and a fire kindled, and says that for at least a mile between Beaulieu Manor and the Forest there was a large settlement of this kind in scattered cottages. The ostensible business of these squatters was to cut furze for the neighbouring lime kilns, but they were, the Rev. William says, really poachers, deer and timber thieves.[2] Near Gilbert White's Selborne, in 1789, the cottages were of good stone or brick, had glazed windows and chambers above stairs.

Few farms in the Isle of Wight did not have cottages attached to them; some tile was used, but more frequently thatch, the walls being plastered and whitewashed inside and the cottages rarely occupied by more than one family, an illuminating remark.[3] These cottages seem to have been substantially built of stone, or, as in Bonchurch,[4] of stone with patches of slate and brick; at Seagrove, H. P. Wyndham,[5] another of our invaluable tourists, notes that the stables only of a gentleman's house had been completed in 1793 and these were fitted up as tenements for poor families.

Dorset towns were mainly built of freestone where it was accessible. Shaftesbury, Sherborne and Lyme Regis were examples.[6] The Isle of Purbeck as well as the quarries near Sherborne supplied stone tiles.[7]

---

[1] Charles Vancouver, *General View . . . Agric. of Hants.* (1813), pp. 63–71.

[2] Rev. William Gilpin, *Remarks on Forest Scenery* (1791), ii, pp. 39, 45. Written before 1781.)

[3] Charles Vancouver, *op. cit.*, pp. 73–4.

[4] J. Hassell, *A Tour of the Isle of Wight* (1790), pp. 666, 668, 670, 688. (Pinkerton's Tours.)

[5] H. P. Wyndham, *A Picture of the Isle of Wight in the Year* 1793 (1794).

[6] Anon, *Rural Elegance Displayed* (1768), p. 259; William George Maton, *Observations on the Western Counties: 1794 and 1796* (1797), ii, p. 11.

[7] William Stevenson, *General View . . . Agric. of Dorset* (1812), p. 86.

The county was noted as one where the number of large farms had increased, and where the farmers occupied small low houses built of stone and covered with slate, usually on a site in a bottom. Many of these were very old and were probably seats of proprietors in former times. The only difference in the more ordinary farmhouses was that they were thatched with reed instead of being tiled with stone or slate. The cottages were more ordinarily of cob on the east of Dorchester, and they were built with a dung fork, having walls 2 ft. thick,[1] while in the dairy district of West Dorset the houses are said by Marshall[2] to be either of stone or cob when he was there in 1791 and 1794. Flint and chalk were used for walls in the chalk district, many cottages in the county having only three rooms and a clay floor in the lower storey. Those who built after the turn of the century found that a cottage with two rooms below and two above under a sloping roof cost about £80, although near Beaminster only £60.[3]

The cottages in Devon met with universal condemnation. Cob was generally used and the optimistic Simond was forced to admit that the villages were not beautiful, the houses being very poor indeed. He finds some consolation in the fact that the windows were generally whole and clean, no old hats or bundles of rags stuck in. On the east of Plymouth he found the walls were partly stone, partly 'pisai', the floors being of cobblestones like the streets. Exmouth at about this time possessed a row of twenty-three elegant brick houses, Alexander Dennis' remark being a sufficient commentary on the generality of buildings.[4] At Tiverton, by 1790, the local historian, Martin Dunsford, makes it clear that a great many houses were built of red brick, many others of stone, but some with earth. Slate was the usual roof excepting those houses that had escaped the last great fire and the poor ones at the edge of the town. A large number of cottages here, no less than sixty-four in the previous sixty years, had fallen to ruin, partly owing to the decline of the woollen industry and partly, says our author, to monopolizing small farms.

Fifty years before Simond's visit Mrs. Powys[5] recorded her impression that the Devon cottages were really meaner than in any country;

[1] John Claridge, ibid. (1793), pp. 24, 31, 83-5.
[2] William Marshall, *Rural Economy of the W. of England* (1796), ii, p. 138.
[3] William Stevenson, *op. cit.*, p. 85.
[4] Alexander Dennis, *Journal of a Tour . . . in . . .* 1810 (1816), p. 8.
[5] Emily J. Climenson (ed.), *Passages from the Diary of Mrs. Philip Lybbe Powys* (1899), p. 206.

they were so poor indeed as to be unsafe, and she tells of a midsummer storm when the rain was so heavy that twenty were demolished and one old lady drowned in her bed, the walls built of a composition of clay and straw being soon broken down. A modern writer on cob, the architect Clough Williams Ellis, does not agree with her. 'There are to-day (1919) plenty of old cob cottages that are damp and insecure, but to condemn cob building in general because certain old builders were careless . . . is to condemn all materials . . . in the same breath.

'In many instances the Devonshire leaseholder, usually only a "life-lease" holder, built badly and on indifferent foundations. He neglected to repair his thatch, with the consequence that ruin followed sooner or later. He did not always use rough-cast, so that it often happened that by the time the lease expired the unfortunate landowner found that the cottage fell in—in the literal as well as the legal sense . . . and the dwelling presented that appearance of squalor and meanness that has led so many to decry the mud buildings of Devon as relics of bygone barbarism.'[1]

Some of the towns, such as Axminster, Upton Pyne and South Zeal in Cornwall, were built of a rugged kind of stone that seemed to wear well. The houses of stone were extremely mean, although Charmouth is allowed by George Lipscombe to have fortunately possessed an air of neatness and comfort in 1799.[2] The farms were almost uniformly small, many being of twenty to forty acres, and not many larger than 200 acres, so that the use of the cheapest possible building material is readily comprehensible.[3] The accommodation was a room about 14 ft. square with a fire-place and oven, two storerooms for fuel and provisions and two rooms upstairs. Many such cottages had fallen into decay largely because of the fragility of the material used in building them, but the developers still adhered to a wall of stone 8 ft. high and cob above that, the Rev. Mr. Luxmoore of Bridestowe having built ninety-five such cottages with one room of 16 ft. square below and a bedroom of about the same size above, about 1800.[4]

[1] Clough Williams Ellis, *Cottage Building in Cob, Pisé, Chalk and Clay* (1919), p. 34.

[2] George Lipscombe, *A Journey into Cornwall* (1799), pp. 142, 166, 344.— W. G. Maton, *op. cit.*, p. 93.

[3] R. Fraser, *General View . . . Agric. of Devon* (1794), p. 17.—William Marshal *Rural Economy of the W. of England* (1796), i, p. 62 *et seq.*, ii, p. 112.

[4] Charles Vancouver, *County Report* (1808), pp. 92–3, 403.

Stebbing Shaw made a tour of the West of England in 1788,[1] and notes when he arrived at St. Austell that its buildings were superior to what he had lately seen, and mostly built of the moorstone of the country mixed with spar and ore, and this is by no means surprising. In Cornwall holdings were small and the almost universal building material was cob, farmhouse and cottage being hardly distinguishable, so meagre was the house room, two rooms below and two above being common to both, although some of the farmhouses were larger, having kitchen, parlour and dairy, with three rooms above. Whole villages, like Sennen, were built of mud, but some modern farmhouses were being built of stone and slate around 1800.[2]

In Somerset the cottagers were no better off, few having more than one room upstairs, while in the middle district the farmhouses were ill-constructed, although the new ones were much improved.[3] Here it was the practice at least near Bridgwater, to cover the fronts of houses with brick tiles to make them weatherproof, and the Rev. Edmund Butcher thought this better than to build of brick;[4] such treatment does, in fact, produce a drier wall. In some places cottages were built of a bluish limestone, called lyas by William George Maton, which abounded about Somerton and Kingsdon, but the majority were of cob between Dulverton and Wiveliscombe.

The whole of the more remote of the south-western counties were poorly housed, with the exception of those farmers who occupied old manor-houses or the new buildings on large holdings, and west of Dorset these were few. So far as the use of cob for building was concerned, it was a question of what was considered economically possible on the smaller holdings, and the same material was widely used elsewhere in the country.

In the Fens of Lincoln and Cambridge cottage building in 1807 had by no means kept pace with farming improvements. Both farmhouse and cottage in these counties were of stud and mud, or lath or plaster,

[1] Rev. Stebbing Shaw, *Tour of the W. of England in 1788* (1789), p. 378.

[2] R. Fraser, *General View . . . Agric. of Devon* (1794), pp. 31, 45.—G. B. Worgan, *General View . . . Agric. of Cornwall* (1811), pp. 23–4, 26.—cf. author of a *Tour in Ireland* (does not read like Young), *Journal of a Tour to the Western Counties . . . in 1807* (1809), p. 20.

[3] J. Billingsley, *General View . . . Agric. of Somerset* (1798), pp. 32, 203.

[4] Rev. Edmund Butcher, *An Excursion from Sidmouth to Chester . . . in 1803* (1805), p. 19.

the cottages only having one room below and one above stairs,[1] although Young gives a plan of a farmhouse costing nearly £1,000 to build and Gooch, another county reporter, admits that Hardwicke's new cottages in Cambridgeshire were good. In contrast to this opulent farmhouse the cost of a stud and mud cottage was only £30, while the new cottages in the enclosed fens when built of brick cost £50 for the smallest size and eighty guineas for a pair.[2] Some fifty years before this, a tourist 'T.G.', in Holland, Lincolnshire, noted that the houses were generally built of brick and their roof covered with tile, slate or reed; those indeed of the meaner sort were of mud. There was no stone house, and none thatched with straw.[3]

A more optimistic view of the conditions in Rutland was taken by Richard Parkinson. Stone was generally used for building, and in the three plans he obtained from the Earl of Winchelsea's steward, the accommodation is normal, two bedrooms and a privy being provided even in the cottage house for labourers.[4] But this must have been the better type of house. Boys of Betteshanger, in Kent, reports that he observed many cottages in the county with walls made entirely of clay, having chimneys of poles daubed inside and outside with the same material, as he says, a very cheap mode of building.[5]

Bedford in 1800 still had some farmhouses and cottages of wattle-and-daub in the north-east, but in the west of the county stone was used, and on the Duke's estates cottages of two, three and four rooms—the average was three—had been built. Here again some farmers were in occupation of what were formerly seats of gentlemen.[6]

Leicester, Northampton and Warwick all had buildings of an inferior sort, probably because the farms in all these counties were on the small side, or rather were of an average that the county reporters regarded as not very large.

On the grazing and breeding holdings of Leicester, however, the

[1] W. Gooch, *Cambridge* (1813), pp. 30–1.—Arthur Young, *General View* ... *Agric. of Lincoln* (1799), pp. 34–6.

[2] Arthur Young, ibid., p. 28 *et seq.*, 35.

[3] Q[uincy] T[homas], *A Short Tour in the Midland Counties in* ... 1772 ... 1774 (1775).

[4] Richard Parkinson, *General View* ... *Agric. of Rutland* (1808), pp. 27–8 and plans.

[5] John Boys, *General View* ... *Agriculture of Kent* (1790), pp. 30–1.

[6] Thomas Batchelor, *General View* ... *Agriculture of Bedford* (1808), pp. 19–21.

houses were built of brick and tile, or other permanent and durable materials, although many in the villages were of timber and plaster walls and the cottages of mud both being thatched. A new cottage erected by Mr. Smith of Ashley-upon-the-Wolds was provided with two bedrooms, a living room and a pantry, with space for a pig to lie. Marshall adds that the ground floors were of paving bricks and the chamber floor of oak, elm or plaster in the farmhouses. The Northampton farmhouses were either of stone or brick and the cottages of the same or inferior materials, a great number being of mud. The majority were thatched and nearly all were situated in the villages, an evidence of their pre-enclosure origin. The county town was built of a reddish stone quarried nearby and Peterborough houses, seen by Resta Patching in 1755, were built of stone and roofed with reeds or coarse slate. The older farmhouses of Warwick also were of timber and mud, or clay walls and thatched roofs: some had stone walls. The more modern were of brick and tile. Where these conditions reigned it is natural to find the older cottages spoken of as miserable hovels, of clay and thatch, but the newer were of stone and thatched or tiled having a large living room and two bedrooms.[1] Naseby was entirely built of earth or mud and is commented on for this characteristic by Samuel Ireland in 1795.

Stafford was rather more fortunate, the modern houses being built of brick or slate or tile, but the omission of any reference to the older buildings is significant. Pitt, the county reporter, gives five plans of farmhouses and cottages. The largest farmhouse cost £1,000–£2,000, the smallest £300–£500. The cottages were on a less ample scale. Two, each with a kitchen, pantry and bedroom on the ground floor, and possibly two bedrooms above, are estimated to cost from £80 to £100. At this time the Rev. Edmund Butcher remarked the brick houses of the one long street at Burton-on-Trent, having only a dirty appearance, but the new cotton factory village of Lea-wood in Nottingham had been built of local stone.[2]

The influence of the newly erected factory villages had, it is suggested, some bearing on rural housing in Derby, where there were many

[1] William Marshall, *Rural Economy of the Midland Counties* (1790), i, p. 26.— W. Pitt, *General View . . . Agric. of Stafford* (1808), pp. 16, 22–5.—ibid., *Gen. View . . . Agric. Northants* (1809), pp. 25–9.—Adam Murray, *Gen. View . . . Agric. Warwick* (1813), pp. 29–31.—See also Simond, *op. cit.*, p. 108.

[2] W. Pitt, *General View . . . Agric. of Staffs.* (1808), p. 29 *et seq.*—Rev. Edmund Butcher, *op. cit.*, pp. 233, 324.

rather small farms occupied by miners. Bricks of a fine colour and texture were made near Derby, but perhaps too much emphasis must not be laid upon the influence of the good cottages erected by Arkwright, Strutt, Oldhouse and others. Still, Farey, in 1815, thought the cottages better than those in the south of England, few being thatched and all being built of stone or brick, like the farmhouses, and with stone or tile roofs.[1]

Farms in the West Riding were generally small, many being in the hands of small freeholders and copyholders. A holding of 100 acres was large; the majority were under 50 acres. The farmhouses were stone with pantile roofs, few of which were to be seen south of Grantham, although Marshall in 1788 states that they were universal north of that place. Young, however, says that the first stone buildings he saw when travelling northwards in 1796 were after leaving Doncaster. Imported deal was used for the woodwork, floors, beams, joists and roofs, oak having been almost wholly laid aside, except for doors, window lintels and wall-plates. Brick had also become a common material in the Vale of Pickering. There was a dearth of cottages for the labourers, most of whom were young, unmarried men, who boarded in the farmhouses. The towns, or rather villages, were also of these substantial materials, the blue slate tiles of Kirby Lonsdale being remarked as picturesque by John Hutton in 1788, and the freestone buildings of Richmond as neat and commodious by Col. Thornton in 1804, although the town was 'as badly paved as Bedale'. The East and North Ridings were not so well accommodated. The mud wall and thatch roofed farmhouse occurred in the East Riding, although by 1794 some had been rebuilt of solid materials and covered with tile. On the Wolds brick or chalk stone were common at that date when the cottages were said to be improving, but when many still had a floor below the ground level and windows which could not be opened. The limestone and mud mortar walls were giving way to brick and pantile by 1812, and the cottages were said to be more comfortable than in many parts of the kingdom, having two lower rooms and two bedrooms above. On the Wolds they were built of chalk and thatched, in the Vale of bricks or mud and pantiles. The farms in the North Riding varied greatly in size, many being in the hands of the 'yeomanry'. The farmer himself was 'by no means well accommo-

[1] Thomas Brown, *General View . . . Agric. of Derby* (1794), p. 14.—W. Hutton, *History of Derby* (1791), p. 12.—W. Farey, *General View . . . Agric. of Derby* (1815), ii, pp. 9-14, 21.

dated', the labourer worse, the cottages having but one room only, two being a rarity.[1]

The four northern counties of Durham, Northumberland, Cumberland and Westmorland had some features in common, although John Bailey could find no more to say of the Durham cottages in 1810 than that they were in general comfortable dwellings of one storey, covered with thatch or tiles and much the same as other districts.[2] It is evident that like many of his contemporaries he did not consider the housing of the labourers a very important matter.

An anonymous traveller who went to Scotland in 1704 was struck by the numerous thatched roofs in Northumberland and mentions Felton, Charleton and Belton in particular. Alnwick was in his eyes a poor straggling town, chiefly thatched. It was rebuilt in the following seventy years because William Hutchinson remarked the buildings as chiefly modern then, but no improvement had taken place in the rural cottages, especially near the borders. 'The cottages of the lower class of people,' says he, 'are deplorable, composed of upright timbers fixed in the ground, the interstices wattled and plastered with mud; the roofs, some thatched and others covered with turf; one little piece of glass to admit the beams of day; and a hearthstone on the ground, for the peat and turf fire. Within there was exhibited a scene to touch the feelings of the heart; description sickens on the subject . . . the damp earth, the naked rafters, the breeze disturbed embers, and distracted smoke that issued from the hearth . . . the midday gloom, the wretched couch, the wooden utensils that scarce retain the name of convenience, the domestic beast that stalls with his master, the disconsolate poultry that mourns upon the rafters, form a group of objects suitable for a great man's contemplation.' Some of these poor dwellings had, however, two rooms, because Mrs. Calderwood was shown into a parlour by a cottager in 1756. In the vales along the Tyne there was a different scene; gentlemen's seats and well-built farmhouses formed the view,

---

[1] William Marshall, *Rural Economy of Yorkshire* (1788), i, p. 106 *et seq.*, 254.—Rennie, Brown and Sherriff, *General View . . . Agric. of the W. Riding* (1794), pp. 15, 24.—W. Brown, *West Riding* (1799), pp. 13, 16.—John Houseman, *Topographical Description of Cumberland, etc.* (1800), pp. 169, 171-2.—John Hutton, *A Tour to the Caves and Ingleborough* (1781, 2nd ed.), p. 7.—Col. T. Thornton, *A Sporting Tour . . . N. of England* (1804), p. 6.—J. Leatham, *General View . . . Agric. of E. Riding* (1794), pp. 27-9.—Mr. Tuke, *ibid.* for *N. Riding* (1794), pp. 19, 80.

[2] John Bailey, *General View . . . Agric. of Durham* (1810), p. 60.

the clay-built cottage and naked-footed poverty being absent. Bailey and Culley could not say anything better in 1797. The old cottages were built of stone and clay and thatched but the modern ones were built of stone and lime and tiled, the floor being formed of lime and sand. These only had one room of 15 ft. by 16 ft. to dwell in and a small one at the entrance for a cow, coals, working tools, etc., of 9 ft. by 16 ft. Such cottages were single storey.[1] Even in a town of 4,000 inhabitants like Morpeth, the houses were low, many of them old and thatched according to the Rev. Wm. MacRitchie in 1795.[2]

The farms in Westmorland and Cumberland were but small; the majority being the property of the smallholders who worked them. In Appleby many of the buildings were ancient but the newer were built of red freestone. Penrith was well-built and by 1773 Sir James Lowther had erected his factory village, 'The Village' of stone, handsomely sashed and covered with blue slate which William Hutchinson found admirable. Ambleside, a straggling little market town in 1791, was made up of rough-cast white houses, and Kendal, a street of a mile long, of the same materials.[3]

John Housman's description of the buildings in the two counties as they were in 1800 amplifies the information in the county reports. In Cumberland, he says, some of the buildings were built of brick, others of clay and mud, but generally with stone. The brick buildings prevail most in market towns and those of clay near the borders of Scotland. Old wooden buildings, like the Guildhall at Carlisle, have now almost disappeared in the north. Most farmhouses, cottages, etc., were straw-thatched and the stone of the walls were laid with clay instead of mortar. This was, I have been informed by Capt. Edwin Gunn, one-time architect to the Ministry of Agriculture, because the local slatestone was impervious to wet and a lime mortar would have absorbed the wet, making the walls damp. A clay mortar was as impervious as the stone. The more modern buildings were slate tiled

[1] North of England, Scotland in MDCCIV (1818), pp. 32–3.—W. Hutchinson, View of Northumberland, Anno. 1766 (1778), ii, p. 244; i, 71, 258.—John Bailey and G. Culley, General View ... Agric. of Northumberland (1797), pp. 27–8.

[2] Rev. William MacRitchie, Diary of a Tour through N. Britain in 1795 (1897).

[3] William Hutchinson, An Excursion to the Lakes ... August 1773 (1774), pp. 40, 50, 57.—A Gentleman, A Tour from London to the Lakes in ... 1791 (1792), pp. 72, 113.

and lime bound . . . in the clay districts modern improvements were considered unnecessary and expensive. Among the mountains away from limestone the houses were built with clay or lime, but were lime-washed inside to keep out the wind. Most of the ancient houses belonging to the common people were extremely simple, consisting of a kitchen and parlour only; 'in the former the family sit, eat and do all their household work; and in the latter they sleep, and sometimes keep their butter, milk and cheese . . . windows are mere pigeon holes'. In the west there were few cottages, as the small farms were worked by the family or by servants who boarded with it. The farmhouses were eight-roomed.[1]

About Westmorland, Housman was enthusiastic. There the buildings were the equal of any in the kingdom. The same conditions obviated the necessity for more cottages.

The mud farmhouse was not very different from that of stone. Such buildings in 1775, according to an anonymous 'Landowner', who was endorsed by Francis Forbes three years later, were occupied by farmers of from £30 to £100 a year in the western and northern counties, and they may be a general pattern of the type, although the generalization is a little façile. A rough stone foundation of from 2 ft. to 3 ft. high was laid, then mud walls of clay or strong loam mixed with water and tempered with straw 16 ft. to 18 ft. high. The rooms were a kitchen 16 ft. by 20 ft., staircase 6 ft. with a buttery behind it, a parlour of 14 ft. by 16 ft. and three 'very inconvenient chambers above'. The floors of the ground storey were either earth or lime ash, or paved with small stones.[2]

Lancashire also was a county of small farms, but it was also a county of the rising manufactures. The farms were as small as 10–50 acres, the majority being between 30 and 50, but in most of the villages there was a larger farm, probably the old demesne varying from 100 to 600 acres in extent. In the north and east the buildings, like those of Cumberland and Westmorland, were roomy and well built of stone and slate, as Mrs. Grant of Laggan, a lover of the picturesque, complains between 1773 and 1807. In the west there was this type of building, but brick and tile were also used, and in the neighbourhood of Garstang and the

[1] John Houseman, op. cit., pp. 50–2.—J. Bailey and G. Culley, General View . . . Agric. of Cumberland (1794), pp. 11–12.—ibid. (1797), pp. 179–80.

[2] A Landowner, Rural Improvements (1775), p. 291. (In this connection Thomas Harding in the Journal of R. Soc. of Arts, 18th Mar., 1927, is interesting.)

VIII COTTAGES AT BRIDESTOWE IN DEVON. (early 19th century)

From Charles Vancouver, *General View of the Agriculture of Devon*, 1808

IX GEORGE MORLAND
(1763–1804)
'Cottage Fireside'

X GEORGE MORLAND: 'HAPPY COTTAGERS'
Clothing probably idealised. The cottage appears to have one room

Fylde, 'clob and clay' with thatch of wheaten straw was found once more, and such houses had seldom more than a ground floor.[1]

The dairy farms of Cheshire were on the average small, ranging between 50 and 100 acres, but there were some few larger farms of 300–500 acres and the houses were built of various materials. Between Congleton and Buxton stone was the building material, but the cottages were few and in the Rev. Edmund Butcher's eyes, 'mean-looking, built of coarse, dark stone', but at about the same time (the end of the century) John Manners, Duke of Rutland, remarks that the houses in most of the Cheshire towns were 'white, with black beams intersecting one another, which has a very curious appearance', although it was only a few years before that it seemed to 'A Gentleman' that 'the grass farms and wooden thatched houses are just what I remember forty years ago, only they look a little older'. The county reporters have nothing to add to this, except that the cottages were not inferior to other counties.[2]

Salop must have resembled other counties, but definite information is meagre. Between Ludlow and Shrewsbury, 'small white cottages' were frequently occurring in 1803 and many old mansions had become farmhouses by that time.[3]

The fortunate counties of Hereford and Worcester were in a different category. Ross, with its famous houses of stone and slate, must have looked much the same 250 years ago as it does to-day. The farmers, however, did not have such substantial buildings. Half a century later Dr. Pococke writes, 'All the old houses in Herefordshire are built with frames of wood and cage-work between called pargiting ...'; not much change was to be remarked at the end of the century. Although the farms were generally pretty extensive, the houses were considered

[1] John Houseman, *op. cit.*, pp. 141–4.—Rev. C. Crutwell, *Tour through Great Britain* (1801), i, cxvii.—Dickson and Stevenson, *General View ... Agric. of Lancs.* (1815), pp. 90, 96, 103–5, 113.—*See also* Louis W. Moffitt, *England on the Eve of the Industrial Revolution* (1925), p. 51 *et seq.*

[2] J. Wedge, *General View ... Agric. of Cheshire* (1794), p. 12.—Henry Holland, ibid. (1808), pp. 83, 86, 93.—Rev. Edmund Butcher, *op. cit.*, p. 216.— John Manners, Duke of Rutland, *Journals of Three Years' Travels ...* 1795–7 (1805), p. 383.—Samuel Johnson, *Diary of a Journey into N. Wales in ...* 1774 (1816), p. 33. (Nantwich: scarcely any but black timber houses.)—A Gentleman, *op. cit.*, p. 23.

[3] Rev. Edmund Butcher, *op. cit.*, p. 152.—Joseph Plymley, *General View ... Agric. of Shropshire* (1803), p. 95.

F

poor, being built with a stone wall a foot or two high, then lath and plaster, the floors being laid with flag tiles; the later buildings were of good brick, stone, etc. The cottages also were of humble and inferior construction, but a row of ten then recently built at Holmer were of brick and timber having one ground floor room 12 ft. by 14 ft. and 6½ ft. high with a shed behind and one room of the same size above. The farms of Worcester were smaller than those of Hereford, but much the same materials were used for building. Some of the new farmhouses were good, but the general part were of ancient construction, badly designed and situated in the villages, often having walls of timber and mortar or plaster. Cottages of the same material and having thatched roofs were 'merely a shelter from the weather', but some new ones erected near Bromsgrove were provided with a living-room, a pantry and two bedrooms above. One pump served the three, as did a common wash and bake house.[1]

Marshall visited Gloucester in 1783 and again in 1788. In the Vale he found the buildings in general of framework plastered or weather boarded, but some walls were of brick and freestone. Slate for roofs had been superseded by knobbed tiles, but cottages and outbuildings were thatched. Floors were formerly of oak, but elm, bricks or stone were then used. In the Cotswolds the buildings were of stone, the timber used was oak and floors were of stone, oak or deal. Practically the same observations were made by Thomas Rudge nearly twenty years later. The old farmhouses, as they decayed, were then being replaced by stone or brick buildings, thatch was giving way to tiles of stone or brick. The floors were still of stone or grip (lime) or brick, but the parlour floor was of oak and bedrooms of elm. The Vale cottages were dilapidated, but building cottages was regarded as an unprofitable investment. 'The greatest of evils to agriculture would be to place the labourer in a state of independence.' In spite of this feeling some good cottages with a lower room 12 ft. by 12 ft. 4 in. and 8 ft. high, two bedrooms 8 ft. by 12 ft. by 8 ft. high, were built on a site near Stow by E. G. Chamberlayne.[2]

All the records go to show that there were widely divergent standards

[1] Dr. Pococke, *Travels through England*, in Camden Soc., new series, xliv, p. 288.—John Clark, *General View . . Agric. of Hereford* (1794), pp. 14, 57.— John Duncumb, *ibid*. (1805), p. 30.—W. T. Pomeroy, *General View . . . Agric. of Worcs*. (1794), p. 9.—William Pitt, ibid. (1813), pp. 19, 22.

[2] William Marshall, *Rural Economy of Gloucs*. (1789), i, pp. 30–7; ii, p. 16.— Thomas Rudge, *General View . . . Agric. of Gloucs*. (1807), pp. 43–50.

of cottage and small farmhouse building in different parts of the country and often in the same neighbourhood during the sovereignty of the four Georges. Much new building had been done, occasionally to the extent of entirely rebuilding a village if it chanced to be wholly the property of a prosperous and improving landowner: but a great many cottages were of inferior and ancient construction everywhere, having poor and limited accommodation. The influence of the economic changes which took place also had a depressive effect, and during the French wars and many years after them the position of the labourer in practically all respects had worsened. Possibly the description of *The Village Labourer* and his circumstances during the war years and until the New Poor Law of 1834, provided by J. L. and Barbara Hammond, is too unrelieved, but it is certain that these circumstances were pretty desperate and that it took nearly a century for them to improve in spite of attempts at palliative legislation by law-makers unpractised in this sort of thing. However, that belongs properly to the next section.

VI   FURNITURE AND CLOTHING

IN the previous section an attempt has been made to give a numerical measure of the furniture and clothing owned by the cottagers of the sixteenth and seventeenth centuries. It is the only answer to the question whether they were adequately outfitted. The almost complete contemporary lack of interest in such questions during the eighteenth century makes the evidence scanty, and it is only with the growth of the philanthropic movement towards 1800 that enquiries were instituted and catalogues prepared of the interior conveniences of cottage homes.

There is fortunately a good deal of indirect evidence, although inventories attached to wills become fewer as time goes on, because the few possessions of the poorer people were not valuable enough to make it worth while to make a will. There are others made for various reasons besides the death of the owner and these are useful. Other satisfactory sources are contemporary engravings and the descriptive passages in contemporary literature.

The inventories of the sixteenth and seventeenth centuries show that the cottagers had no great range of goods and chattels. In the eighteenth a man who in the earlier time was worth £100 and upwards was most likely much richer and so further away from the cottager. The eighteenth century homes described here must be taken to be more akin, and increasingly so, as time progresses, to the labourer in depression from the opening of the French wars until the Great War of 1914-18.

As to pictures, Morland's 'Innocence alarmed, or The Flash in the Pan' shows a cottage living room with three pewter plates on the mantel-shelf, two drop leaf tables, two hams hanging from the ceiling (a wealth of food). The floor is tiles or bricks, probably the latter. One fire dog is visible, the woman being busy lighting a fire with branches.

Such pictures are confirmed by the extant documents. One is preserved in East Dean Church, Sussex. It is a rough inventory of chattels sold when Dame Battlemore died and is late eighteenth century. Her effects were one bolster, etc., presumably other bed furniture, six chairs, a cradle, a table, a teakittle, a frypan, three old shelves, a grid-iron, an old skillet, a tub, a pewter mortar and a coffer. Unsold were a boiler, a small bedstead, six glass bottles, one rumor (? rummer), a handbill and axe, tongs and a jug, and another illegible article.

It seems that when anyone applied for poor relief it was customary for the overseers to make an inventory of the applicant's goods, and J. Hambley Rowe has printed two from a rate book dating from 1747 in the *Bradford Antiquary*.[1] These were of women who came on the rates. Ann Whiticker of Cowling had two tables, a chest, a cofer, three chairs, two stools, a wheel (? spinning), a reel, one iron pan, a bread pan, a bedstead with a chaff bed, two blankets, a quilt and two bolsters; Martha Snowden of Stubin in Cowling, one chest, two chairs, two wheels, a reel, a pair of tongs, a table, a potcase, a pair of bellows, bedstead and chaff bed, two blankets, one rug, three bolsters, and a quantity of pots.

Another pauper, Thomas Barber, died at Meldreth, Cambridge, in 1702. If he really was a pauper his goods include some refinements. They were, one featherbed, one flockbed, two feather boulsters, one flock bolster, three pillowes, one blanket, one coverlet, an old rugge, two bedsteads, one old sheet, two pillow bears, two shirts, three curtains and valences. Twelve diaper napkins, one diaper tablecloth, in the chamber two Hutches, two little tables, two boxes, five glass bottels, a mug, a bible, a barrel and 'stok'. In the house or hall four pewter dishes and one plate, two porringers, a salter, a sugging (? sucking) bottle, a flagon, a tin candlestick, a tin pot, an iron candlestick, three kittles, a brass mortar, a warming pan, a frying pan, a lock iron and two padds, a pott-hanger, a pair of tongs, bellows, three wooden dishes, a brass spoon, four trenchers, two glass porringers, two blew plates, a look in glass, a cup-board, a table, one joynted stool, a water pale, five chairs, good and bad, a form, a linen wheel, a heyhook, one suit of clothes. 'A look in glass' for a man who only had one suit of clothes is surely a superfluity, and diaper napkins and tablecloths are certainly unusual possessions for a pauper, but the word may only mean that he was a poor man when he died, or indeed only that he was a labourer.[2]

Another 'pauper's' goods were listed by the parish of Bottisham Load, Cambridgeshire, in 1782. He was John Piper and his bedstead, fether bed, bolster, pillow, one sheet, two blankets and quilt were

[1] Vol. vi (new series iv), 1921, p. 149.

[2] W. N. Palmer, *Meldreth Parish Records* (1896), p. 41.

worth £1 10s. of a total of £3 8s. 2d. Among the other goods were two tea pots and tea kettle, signs in contemporary eyes, of the degeneracy of the times, one obel (oval ?) table, a deal table, seven chairs, a hutch and a cubberd, seven earthen plates and six earthen dishes, two pots, three candlesticks, a buffet stool, a flock bed, pillow and two blankets, a large iron pot, a smaller one, a bucket and pail, a pair of pothooks, a trunk, a glass beker, and a pint bason.[1]

A Cheshire farmer, Thomas Furber, who kept an account of all things he bought when he set up house, in 1767, spent £25 odd on household goods, so he was quite above the modest standard of the 'pauper'. William Crownall, who died in Derbyshire, in 1705, left six pewter dishes, one brass pot, three beetles, one pint flagon, one pewter candlestick, two cubords and one disbord. His parlour contained one table, two bedsteads and three blankets, three sheets, one good pair of sheets and a pillabere, one other little table; his chamber, one chest, one cofer, one boke (a learned man) and a peece of cloth.[2]

Far away from here, A. K. Hamilton Jenkin says that the furniture of the one downstairs room of a Cornish cottage in the eighteenth century was a rude table, and some people had three or four straight backed chairs, although the majority used a long form and a three-legged stool. The children sat on blocks of wood. For the rest there were a few earthenware cups, saucers and basins, some wooden or tin plates, an iron crock for boiling and a kettle or baker.[3] This is confirmed by Simond whose curiosity drove him into rooms in the villages between Exeter and Taunton, where he saw 'a few seats in the form of short benches, a table or two, a spinning wheel, a few shelves, and just now (Christmas, 1814) greens hanging about'.[4]

The possessions of decamping husbands are recorded in the Sessions papers of some counties and Elizabeth W. Gilboy has examined them. These show that the small farmer was probably better equipped than the three poor widows and the 'paupers', although strict comparison is not possible because the detailed inventory of Andrew Clark, of New Brentford, Middlesex, is not given. He is described as a labourer, but the number and kind of his household goods makes it probable he was

[1] E. M. Hampson, *The Treatment of Poverty in Cambridgeshire*, 1597–1834 (1934), p. 296.

[2] W. B. Mercer, *Thomas Furber, an Eighteenth Century Cheesemaker* in *Reaseheath Review* (1933), x.

[3] A. K. Hamilton Jenkin, *Cornwall and its People* (1945), p. 339.

[4] L. Simond, *op. cit.*, p. 12.

something more, especially when it is compared with the inventory of a Plompton, W.R. Yorks, husbandman of 1728, also given. The much less valuable inventories taken in Kent in 1754 and 1761 resemble those of the poor widows and paupers, as does that of John Brooke of Liversidge (W.R.), who also vanished in 1728. A Warwickshire yeoman died in 1706 and left much the same kind and quantity of things.[1]

These conditions obtained well into the nineteenth century. George Eliot, an enthusiast for the older times, writes in *Scenes of Clerical Life*: 'Dorcas had led the way into the best kitchen, as charming a room as best kitchens used to be in farmhouses which had no parlours—the fire reflected in a bright row of pewter plates and dishes; the salt coffer in one chimney corner, and a three-cornered chair in the other, the walls behind handsomely tapestried with flitches of bacon and the ceiling ornamented with pendant hams.' This is riches beyond those of the labourer, but William Howitt, *The Rural Life of England* (1838) proclaims resoundingly that this is no isolated example. 'Let those who doubt it,' he says, 'go into the Dales of Yorkshire; into the Peak and retirements of Derby; into the vales of Nottinghamshire and midland counties; let them traverse Buckinghamshire and Shropshire; let them go into the wild valleys of Cornwall; ay, into the genuine country of almost any part of England, and they will find stone floors, and naked tables, and pewter plates, and straw beds, and homely living enough in all conscience. . . . The spots are not difficult to be found even now, where the old oak table, with legs as thick and black as those of an elephant, is spread in the homely house-place . . .', words almost repeated by Richard Jefferies nearly fifty years later in *Round About a Great Estate*.

Contemporary fiction shows that such rooms as can be envisaged from Dame Battlemore's sale of goods were a commonplace of rural living. A small public house, the Black Lion, on the Great North Road, described by Smollett in *The Adventures of Sir Launcelot Greaves* (1760), had only one room, the kitchen, for entertainment. It was paved with red bricks, remarkably clean, furnished with three or four Windsor chairs, adorned with shining plates of pewter, and copper saucepans, nicely scoured . . .; while a cheerful fire of sea-coal blazed in the chimney. Moritz describes a similar Inn kitchen at Nettlebed near Henley, and a similar parlour kitchen was occupied by *The Vicar of Wakefield* and his family when they fell into reduced circumstances. It was 'kept with

[1] Elizabeth W. Gilboy, *Wages in Eighteenth Century England* (1934), pp. 60-1, 129, 209.

the utmost neatness, the dishes, plates and coppers being well scoured, and all disposed in bright rows on the shelves, the eye was agreeably relieved and did not want richer furniture'. The Vicar's income of £40 a year was, however, at least four times that of a labourer.

The kitchen of Shakespeare's birthplace was inhabited when Samuel Ireland visited it in 1795. The floor was stone flagged, there was a settle in the chimney, a wooden dresser, and mugs and pots on the shelf over the chimney, and a basket hung from a nail in a beam.

An idealized version of a cottage kitchen of this type has been reconstructed and is shown at the Geffrye Museum. It has an open grate with dogs and fireback, a pothanger and large pot, a rush holder, tongs, a ladle and perforated gridle. On the mantelshelf was a candlestick, hourglass, teapot and caddy: on the hearth a trivet and bellows. An oak chest carried a napkin press. The built-in cupboard held delft plates and pewter. There were two chairs and a corner cupboard and in addition a spinet, an improbable piece of furniture in most cottages, especially if this list is compared with Cowper's lines from *The Task*:

> *All the care*
> *Ingenious parsimony takes, but just*
> *Saves the small inventory, bed and stool,*
> *Skillet and old carved chest, from public sale.*

This small inventory is reproduced in Fielding's description of Molly Seagrim's bedroom; it was a garret, 'being up one pair of stairs, that is to say at the top of the house, was of a sloping figure, resembling the great Delta of the Greeks . . . it was impossible to stand upright anywhere except in the middle. Now as this room wanted the convenience of a closet, Molly had, to supply that defect, nailed up an old rug against the rafters of the house, which enclosed a little hole, where her best apparel, such as the remains of that sack . . . some caps, and other things with which she had lately provided herself, were hung up and secured from the dust: this enclosed space exactly fronted the foot of the bed, to which indeed the rug hung so near that it served in a manner to supply the want of curtains'.

Scattered up and down the country are many old farmhouses and cottages and, in spite of modern alterations to the buildings and changes in the furniture, many of them are little different from what they always were. If the modern additions are eliminated some idea of the appearance of the rooms and the comfort of their furniture in the eighteenth century can be obtained. This method has been adopted by Gertrude Jekyll, who provides pictures of farmhouse and cottage kitchens in West Sussex, Kent and Herefordshire and describes them in her *Old English Household Life*. H. Allsopp also describes, in his *The Change to Modern England* (1922), two interiors painted by Sir David Wilkie about 1800.

In the older cottages a brick oven for baking bread was built half in, half outside the wall. The sheet iron door was inside and fitted with two handles for lifting it out. The finished loaves were removed with an oven peel. The south-western counties used, according to Dr. Pococke, 'Clonmel ovens, which are earthenware of several sizes, and being heated, they stop them up and cover them over with embers to keep in the heat; and in the very western parts they have pot ovens, a round piece of iron which is heated, on which the bread is put, and then it is covered over with a pot, on which they heap the embers to keep in the heat'.

The general impression gained from these contemporary pictures is that the articles owned were the minimum necessary for living, but it must be remembered that a steady drift of discarded furniture would find its way from the great houses, as fashions and taste changed, into the less pretentious farmhouses and from them perhaps to the cottages. The heavy oak beds, chairs and tables of earlier times thus came into the important farmhouses and were there supplemented by unpretentious oak-panelled cupboards and dressers of local make, more or less traditional in design, but seldom in the contemporary taste of the wealthy classes. Thence possibly as the fashion for mahogany reached the richer farmers they descended to the cottage.

Unfortunately the evidence about clothing is as, or more, limited than for the earlier times. There is sufficient about clothes as costume, but little in the way of a quantitative measure telling the number of hats and coats a man had. The tourists only remark upon clothing as different from what they were used to. For instance, Muralt[1] at the end of the seventeenth century said that he knew the English peasants but by one way: they 'are commonly on Horseback, in Riding Coats and Plush Breeches, booted and spurred and always galloping. The People in general are well cloathed, which is a certain proof of their living at Ease; for in England the Belly always takes place of the Back'.

[1] Beat, Louis de Muralt, *Letters describing the Character and Customs of the English and French Nations* (1726), p. 10.

The contemporary poet, like the painter, was concerned with appearance. William Shenstone[1] describes a rustic maiden:

> *Her cap, far whiter than the driven snow,*
> *Emblem right meet of decency does yield:*
> *Her apron dy'd in grain, as blue, I trowe,*
> *As the hare-bell that adorns the field.*
>
> *A russet stole was o'er her shoulders thrown;*
> *A russet kirtle fenc'd the nipping air;*
> *Twas simple russet, but it was her own;*
> *Twas her own county bred the flock so fair;*
> *Twas her own labour did the fleece prepare.*

John Clare also occasionally mentions clothes.

> *Now homeward-bound, the hedger bundles round*
> *His evening faggot, and with every stride*
> *His leathern doublet leaves a rustling sound.*

And again,

> *My love she wears a cotton plaid,*
> *A bonnet of the straw. . . .*

The novelists are really not much more explicit. Smollett, describing in *Joseph Andrews* a country youth with hopes above his station, says he 'went constantly dressed as fine as could be, with two clean Holland shirts a week', and a country girl dressed for her wedding could 'attire herself in nothing richer than a white dimity nightgown. . . . She wore one of her own short round-eared caps and over it a little straw hat, lined with cherry coloured silk, and tied with a cherry-coloured riband'. But also in *Sir Launcelot Greaves* the buxom country lasses were 'in the best apparel dight, their white hose, and clean short dimity petticoats, their gaudy gowns of printed cotton, their top-knots and stomachers, bedizened with bunches of ribbons of various colours, green, pink and yellow'. Not much more information is to be derived from pictures, and in any case the condition of the clothing is probably idealized in them, except in caricature, like Hogarth, where it would tend to be depicted in exaggerated decay.

Peculiarities of costume in different districts have been widely

---

[1] William Shenstone, *Poems* (*c.* 1745).

commented upon. The use of pattens by the women was probably general. Kalm remarks upon them in Essex where women on a visit leave them in the passage. They were also used in Sussex. Pattens were a wooden shoe which stood on a high iron ring and were worn over the ordinary leather or stuff shoe. They served to keep the wearer out of the mud. In the north-western counties foreigners were impressed by shoes with wooden soles. These were habitual in Cumberland, Westmorland and north Lancashire in 1750.[1] Many people wore them without stockings on working days. The utility of such shoes was not considered by a writer in the *Annals of Agriculture* for 1793, who thought them a sign of the poverty resulting from high wages and the low price of spirituous liquors, which were used immoderately.

In Kent, Kalm was entertained to see every male, farm-servant, clodd-hopper, day-labourer, farmer, going about his usual everyday duties with a peruque on his head, very few wearing their own hair. And the people in the Home Counties must have been well dressed if his description of an English countrywoman's dress on a visit was at all usual. They commonly wore a red cloak, and the pattens over their ordinary shoes. 'All go laced and wear for every day use a sort of Manteau, made commonly of brownish camlot. The same headdress as in London. Here it is not unusual to see a farmer's or other small personage's wife, clad on Sunday like a lady of "quality" at other places in the world and her everyday attire in proportion. "Paniers" are seldom used in the country. When they go out they always wear straw hats, which they have made themselves from wheat straw, and are pretty enough. On high days they have on ruffles.'

A few years later, 1765, M. Grosley[2] remarked upon the comfort in which the Kent labourers were clothed. Each driver of some waggons loaded with corn was dressed in good cloth, a warm great coat upon his back, and good boots upon his legs, and these drivers rode upon a little nag, not on the waggon. At Wellen (Welwyn), Hertfordshire, another foreigner, Jeanne-Marie Philipson Roland, was surprised because the women never went out without hats, 'which is mostly black for those of the common class, often gathered in behind like a bonnet'. It was the 'poke' bonnet, worn over a handkerchief or cap. He adds 'the lower sort of women have generally a black stuff petticoat under their coloured cotton gown; large silk handkerchiefs, common red or brown, well extended, and entirely covering the neck,

[1] Pococke, *op. cit.*, p. 44.
[2] M. Grosley, *A Tour to London, or new Observations on England* (1772), p. 17.

the shoulders and the back'.[1] Near Chichester, in Sussex, Thomas Pennant[2] saw well-dressed female peasants in 1801. The young were in grey petticoats, the elder in sober black, and the men were clad in smock frocks over their clothes and often mounted on pretty ponies.

Adam Bede's mother, who was supposed to have been alive in 1799, was garbed much as the peasant women described. 'Her grey hair is turned neatly back under a pure linen cap with a black band round it; her broad chest is covered with a buff neckerchief, and below this you see a sort of short bed gown made of blue-checkered linen, tied round the waist and descending to the hips, from whence there is a considerable length of linsey-wolsey petticoat.' Thirty years before women in the south-west were not so fully clothed. Then the country women near Tiverton never wore gowns except on a Sunday, and even on that day took them off immediately after church. They were all in plaited sleeves and tight stays if we may believe a writer in the *Annals of Agriculture*, 1797, whose evidence is confirmed by Fanny Burney. In her eyes the women's dress was barbarous. 'They have stays half-laced, and something by way of handkerchief about their necks; they wear a single coloured flannel or stuff petticoat, no shoes or stockings . . . and their coat (i.e. upper skirt) is pinned up in the shape of a pair of trousers leaving them naked to the knee.' The habit of not wearing shoes and stockings, added to their general appearance, was taken by some observers to indicate the poverty of the people. These rustic fashions, though they must have been usual in Cornwall, did not obtain everywhere in the county. The Camelford wenches were said by the Rev. Richard Warner to be dressed in the pink of fashion in 1808, and made a whimsical contrast between their fashionable attire and the wretched hovels in which the fine folk dwelt.

These observations afford a fairly complete picture of the appearance of the people in different parts of the country during the Georgian period, but fail to provide any measure of their possessions in clothing. There is, indeed, little evidence on this point. Nobody seems to have had the necessary impertinence, even in that age of curiosity, to ask how many pairs of breeches or shirts a man had, nor the number of caps or petticoats the women owned; or, if they did, they failed to record this very relevant information.

From other sources a little may be gathered. One is the hiring agreement for a servant in Yorkshire, dated 1703. Joseph Mawde was hired

[1] *The Works of Jeanne-Marie Philipson Roland* (1800), p. 173.

[2] Thomas Pennant, *Journey from London to the Isle of Wight* (1801), p. 102.

by Sir Walter Calverley to serve him for one year at a wage of £5 'and 20s. to buy him a frock with for brewing, and a livery vizt. coat breeches hat and stockings'. Presumably he provided his own shirts and shoes or perhaps had them from a previous employment. This servant by the nature of his duties was a handy man and it is evident that these garments were expected to last him for the term of his employment. There is a hiatus even here because Mawde must have had some clothes when hired and we do not know what they were. Probably the livery was really a very considerable addition to his wages, because John Dyer, the writer of the *Fleece* in 1735, states his opinion that 'the poorer and most industrious People, are not cloathed above once in two Years, suppose that Cloathing to cost five Pounds'.

His opinion may have been exaggerated. Young examined the budget of a Lincolnshire family in 1771 and records it with the warning that he does not know how far it applied peculiarly to Lincolnshire. It shows that the man bought a coat, waistcoat and breeches each year for £1 2s., a hat and three pairs of stockings cost 3s. and three shirts 10s. Two pairs of shoes costing 8s. made his annual expenditure on clothes £2 3s. His wife and two children spent just double that but no details are given.

Both Eden (*State of the Poor*) and Davies (*Case of the Labourers, etc.*) worked on more or less modern lines and have left us the kind of information necessary. They only deal with conditions towards 1800, but as there is no other evidence of the same kind, their records must be accepted. Davies' accounts are those of families fairly well distributed over the country and relate to labourers only: but it must be admitted the inquiries he conducted at Barkham, in Berkshire appear to form a basis for many of his other estimates. A characteristic annual supply of clothing for a man was, two shirts, a pair of shoes, two pairs of wooden shoes, a hat and a handkerchief (for the neck) and three pairs of stockings. The main garments are not mentioned. The woman's wardrobe was a gown and petticoat, two shifts, two aprons, a pair of shoes, a pair of wooden shoes, and handkerchiefs. At Holwell, in Somerset, there was a family with six children. The man bought each year a coat and breeches, two pairs of shoes, shirts costing 8s. and stockings 3s. The woman bought a gown and petticoats, shifts for 7s., shoes for 3s. 9d., stockings for 1s. 6d., an apron, caps and handkerchiefs for 6s. The children most likely wore the cast off and cut down garments of their parents. Similar quantities are tabulated for a second family, and Miss Gilboy's examination of the Sessions Papers shows that in 1711 and onwards some country people had spare suits, dresses, etc., that were stolen. Cases occur in Kent and Surrey and in the south-west.

At Auckland, in Durham, the man had much the same as he of Holwell, and his wife had a gown, a petticoat, two shifts, shoes and their repair, two pairs of stockings, two aprons and two caps. The children in this family had shoes, a pair of stockings, coats or gown petticoats one each or one shirt each according to sex. At Affpiddle, in Dorset, the labourers were so poor that they spent nothing on clothes. 'Clothes they get as they can, and the children go nearly naked' is a sufficient commentary. In the Cornish budgets the man is only allowed 5s. a year for the wear of a suit, comprising a jacket and breeches He also had two shirts, a pair of stout shoes, a pair of stockings, a hat and a handkerchief. The woman is allowed the wear of a gown and petticoats, one shift, a pair of strong shoes, one pair of stockings, two aprons, handkerchiefs, caps, etc., and the same allowance is made both at St. Austell and Anthony in the east. Here also an illuminating remark is appended. 'Few poor people bestow upon themselves the sums here supposed.' Davies therefore considers that the children's clothing may reasonably be included within the sums allowed for their parents.

Eden supplies a generalization. 'In the midland and southern counties the labourer, in general, purchases a very considerable proportion, if not the whole, of his cloathes, from the shopkeeper. In the vicinity of the metropolis, working people seldom buy new cloathes: they content, themselves with a cast off coat, which may usually be purchased for about 5s. and secondhand waistcoats and breeches. Their wives seldom make up any article of dress, except making and mending cloathes for the children. In the north, on the contrary, almost every article of dress worn by farmers, mechanics and labourers, is manufactured at home, shoes and hats excepted. . . . Although broadcloth purchased in the shops begins now to be worn by opulent farmers and others on Sundays, yet there are many respectable persons, at this day, who never wore a bought pair of stockings in their lives. . . .' This is confirmed by the Sessions Papers for the North and West Ridings. Eden also describes how the Cumberland labourer was dressed. He wore a hat, a cloth coat and waistcoat, a pair of leather breeches, although they sometimes wore breeches of flannel or coloured cloth, a linen shirt, stockings and shoes. The women wore a black stuff hat, a linen bedgown, stamped with blue, and home made, a cotton or linen neckcloth, two flannel petticoats, the upper one dyed blue, coarse home-made woollen stockings and a linen shift. They generally wore stays or rather a boddice, and occasionally woollen gowns. On Sundays they wore black silk hats and cotton gowns.

He suggests that near London the things bought annually, unless they will last longer, were: man—a good foul weather coat, will last very well two years, common waistcoat, a pair of stout breeches, a pair of stockings, one dowlas shirt, a pair of strong shoes, a hat, will last two years: woman—a common stuff gown, linsey woolsey petticoat, a shift, a pair of shoes, coarse apron, check apron, a pair of stockings, a hat (the cheapest sort will last two years), coloured neck handkerchief, common cap, cheapest kind of cloak will last two years, a pair of stays will last six years. And he supports this estimate by the real budget of a family living at Hinksworth, Hertfordshire. The man had a stout coat which should last him two years, as should his waistcoat. Breeches required replacing once a year. He had two pairs of stockings and two shirts, a pair of shoes and mending them annually, while his hat was supposed to last him for three years. His wife had a common stuff gown, the cheapest kind of cloak, a petticoat, two shifts, two pairs of shoes, a coarse and a check apron, two pairs of stockings, a hat that was renewed every two years, and a pair of stays that should last her for six years. She also possessed a coloured neck handkerchief and two common caps.

These are quantitative measures and may be accepted as a general criterion of the situation of the poorer classes of rural society. They make the picture as complete as seems possible. While there are few enough detailed statements of the actual possessions of the cottager, there are enough to establish the minimum at a time when the labourers were growing steadily more depressed—the last years of the eighteenth century and the first quarter of the nineteenth. That is as much as can safely be said.

Simond,[1] describing the labourers at Albury, Surrey, in 1815, supplies a useful gloss on their appearance. 'The peasants look very decent in their manners, dress and appearance. No marks of poverty about them; but they are certainly very diminutive in stature and thin. They seem better clothed than fed. One might suspect a certain native pride in them disdains to wear the livery of poverty although they suffer in secret.'

A few remarks on the fuel used for cooking and heating may be a further indication of the way of cottage life in rural England during

[1] L. Simond, *Journal of a Tour in Great Britain* [in 1810–11] (1815), p. 222.

this hundred odd years. For London and its environs the evidence of *The Present State of England* (1750) seems valid. 'Pit coal is most universal,' it runs, 'and is used in open fires.' At such places as Woodford, Essex, some coal was used. It was bought in London and carted there, but even so near London as this, wood was mostly used; in Hertford many of the poorer people gathered bracken and said that it gave in the burning much stronger heat than many kinds of wood. Ellis, indeed, told Kalm that the poor folk used to collect the leaves that fall down from the trees, dry them, and use for fuel, so that some part of their preference for bracken was because it cost nothing. In the later years of the century the new canals allowed coal to be carried to districts where it had previously been unknown. One such was the Stafford canal, which allowed Willoughby, in Leicester, to burn coal after it was built, instead of the dung the village had formerly been forced to rely upon.

This habit of using dung for fuel, to the detriment of the manuring of the land, was fairly widespread, and in remote districts continued to the end of the century. In Portland there was great scarcity of fuel and Dr. Pococke[1] notes that the people made up cow dung mixed with straw and put it in cakes against the walls of their houses to dry for fuel. This practice was still necessary here in 1800, when it was also usual in some parts of Cornwall, Edward Daniel Clarke[2] declaring that an old woman followed their horses with a basket in the hope of adding to her supplies. Edward Laurence[3] advised in 1727 that dung should not be permitted to be used for fuel as it was in Yorkshire and Lincoln and Resta Patching[4] noticed the Portland method of drying the material in Leicester in 1755.

Peat also was a substitute for coal or wood. Halifax produced coal for its industries and the neighbouring parishes were able to supply it, but any deficiency of coal was made up by the plenty of turf earth which some parishes prepared for fuel by drying in the sun. This was reckoned a particularly healthy fuel and it was said that where it was used pestilential disorders were more rare and less fatal. Cambridge was particularly favoured in 1765. Coals were from 7*d.* to 9*d.* a bushel, turf, or rather peat, was 4*s.* a thousand, and sedge which the bakers used

[1] *Op. cit.*, p. 93.

[2] Edward Daniel Clarke, *Tour through the S. of England* ... 1791 (1793), p. 116.

[3] Edward Laurence, *The Duty of a Steward to his Lord* (1727).

[4] R[esta] P[atching], *Four topographical Letters* ... (1757), p. 6.

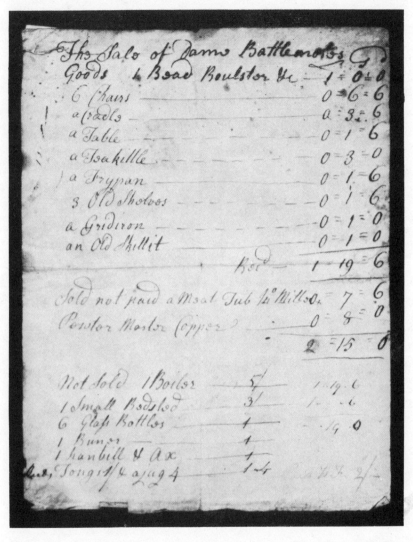

The Sale of Dame Battlemore's
Goods   a Bead Boulster &c. ―――― 1 = 0 = 0
  6 Chairs ―――――――――――― 0 = 6 = 6
  a Cradle ――――――――   a = 3 = 6
  a Table ――――――――――   0 = 1 = 6
  a Teakille ――――――――   0 = 3 = 0
  a Frypan ――――――――――   0 = 1 = 6
  3 Old Sholves ――――――――   0 = 1 = 6
  a Gridiron ――――――――――   0 = 1 = 0
  an Old Skillit ――――――――   0 = 1 = 0
                 Rec   1 - 19 = 6

Sold not paid a Meat Tub Mr Millso = 7 = 6
Pewter Mester Copper   0 = 8 = 0
                            2 = 15 = 0

Not Sold 1 Boiler ――――   5/   1 . 19 . 6
  1 Small Bedstead   3/   1 - . 6
  6 Glass Bottles   t   - 19 . 0
  1 Burner   t
  1 hanbill & Ax   t
  Tongist & a jug 4   1-4   2/-

XI INVENTORY OF DAME BATTLEMORE'S POSSESSIONS
Late 18th century, written on a sheet of notepaper (reduced)

XII HOME OF
GEORGE CRABBE'S
FATHER
c. 1754

From an edition of
his poems, 1834

to heat their ovens, was 4s. a hundred sheaves. Peat was used in Wilt-shire by the cottagers down to 1840, when it was brought mainly from the New Forest, and it even went so far as Salisbury Plain. Before then it was cut near Newbury, Berkshire, and elsewhere and the improbable reason for its use in 1778 was that wood had become scarce and coal was dear. On the borders of Devon and Cornwall furze and brake were collected from the common waste and this must have been the means of supplying heat for cooking and warmth for comfort in a large number of villages all over the country.

Sources of water supply remained as they always had—wells, streams, ponds and roof catchment—except in such fortunate and fairly large towns as Shrewsbury, where a supply was brought into the town by wooden pipes. Pennant says that Chester had a waterworks in 1773. Another method of supplying villages was that used at Honiton. The principal street was 'remarkably paved, forming a small channel well shouldered up on each side with pebles and clean turf which holds a stream of clear water with a square dipping opposite each door; a mark of cleanliness and convenience'. The Rev. Stebbing Shaw[1] had never seen this before 1788. Such a supply must have been extremely susceptible to pollution.

Lighting was most probably very largely confined to rush lights in the cottages. They were made by the cottagers on a method which has been fully described by Gilbert White[2] and must have been the same all over the country. Candles were the prerogative of a wealthier class or at the most very sparingly used.

[1] Op. cit., p. 442.
[2] Gilbert White, Natural History of Selborne.

G

VII FOOD

LEGENDARY history is rarely so apparent anywhere else as it is in discussion of people's food. Feasts are easier to remember than the orderly procession of normal days; cake is more memorable than bread and its recipes more extensive in cookery books; meat more than bacon and game than meat, so that it is difficult for contemporaries to record anything but the festivals.

Real evidence of the constituents, and especially the amount of each, that went to make up the cottager's ordinary meals is difficult to come by for the Tudor and Stuart period, but a datum line is supplied for conditions under the Georges by the workhouse and prison dietaries that were recorded then. It might be assumed that these were less sumptuous than the food enjoyed at home, but no cottager of the day would have agreed. On the contrary, many have said that they got better food in gaol or in the workhouse than at home, and continued to say so until 1850.

A much quoted generalization was made by Eden. He compares the diet of north and south to the disadvantage of the latter. 'In the south, he says, 'the poorest labourers are habituated to the unvarying meal of dry bread and cheese from week's end to week's end: and in those families whose finances do not allow them the indulgence of malt liquor, the deleterious produce of China constitutes their most usual and general beverage. If a labourer is rich enough to afford himself meat once a week, he commonly adopts the simplest of all culinary preparations; that of roasting it; or, if he lives near a baker's, of baking it; and if he boils his meat he never thinks of forming it into a soup, that would be not only as wholesome and as nourishing, but certainly more palatable than a plain boiled joint.'

In the northern counties, on the contrary, the labourers' wives were more competent cooks, and provided their families with hasty puddling, crowdie, frumenty (made of barley), pease-kail and a dish known as lobscouse. They had also many different sorts of bread, both oats and barley being used, as aforetime, and the mixture of rye and wheat, known as maslin as well. Moreover most families baked their own bread and stews were also made. Milk was obtained more easily by the 'poor' in the north because they often kept cows and this was impossible in the south.

This, like most generalizations, is only partly true. The diet of the northern labourer was not always and invariably better than that of the southern, and at any rate in the early part of the eighteenth century some of the things used were common to both: Gay's *Shepherd's Week* makes this clear.

> *In good roast beef my landlord sticks his knife*
> *The capon fat delights his dainty wife,*
> *Pudding our Parson eats, the Squire loves hare*
> *But white-pot thick is my Buxoma's fare . . . .*

Again Marion adopts a hortatory attitude to 'her man'—

> *When hungry thou stoods't staring like an Oaf,*
> *I slic'd the luncheon from the barley loaf,*
> *With crumbled bread I thicken'd well thy mess,*
> *Ah, love me more, or love thy pottage less!*

Robert Bloomfield in *The Farmer's Boy* suggests that the barley loaf was common in Northampton in the lines,

> *A barley loaf, 'tis true, my table crowns,*
> *That, fast diminishing in lusty rounds,*
> *Stops Nature's cravings;*

And W. H. Hudson[1] met an old Hampshire woman in 1902 who told him that the same things were common in that county when she was a girl. But before making a detailed survey it will be well to consider the workhouse and prison diets that the labourers said were better than their home feeding. The accounts are detailed, well spread about the country and widely distributed as to date. Bristol supplied inmates with three meals a day in 1700 and the girls' diet was as mixed, including greenstuff in season, as could reasonably be expected then. *An Account of Several Workhouses* in 1725 includes St. Mary's, White-chapel, where paupers got 1 lb. of bread and 2 oz. of cheese daily,

---

[1] W. H. Hudson, *Hampshire Days* (1923), p. 301.

2½ lb. of meat and 14 pints of beer a week; in addition milk porridge, peas-porridge, beef broth or burgow was supplied. A similar regimen was common to all the workhouses in the *Account*. Cabbage, carrots, turnips, and other vegetables were provided as the season allowed. Meat was served two, three or four days a week in the different places.

Commenting upon the eligible circumstances of the paupers in the Cosford, Suffolk, House of Industry, in 1788, the Rev. Mr. Mills of Hitcham sets out their daily food, which keeps them, he says, in constant readiness for toil or sport, 'as you may be convinced by reading the following bill of fare'. This included unvarying bread and cheese for supper and broth or milk for breakfast. Sunday dinner was seed cake and on three other days bread and cheese, but on Mondays and Fridays dinner was meat dumplings and garden stuff. Wednesday's dinner was plum or suet pudding at the inmate's request. They preferred it to the meat formerly supplied them—an interesting commentary on the habits of the poor or the quality of the meat. The Reverend adds that these people, who are 'living in comparative plenty to what they formerly experienced in the miserable cottages of famished poverty, have strength, health and spirits to finish their light labour'. George Crabbe, who came from this part of the country, did not share this optimism, at any rate about such 'Houses'—

> Theirs is yon House that holds the parish poor,
> Whose walls of mud scarce bear the broken door;
> There, where the putrid vapours, flagging, play,
> And the dull wheel hums doleful through the day . . . .

The Norwich workhouse gave 12 oz. of cheese and 3½ oz. of butter to each person weekly. Meat was 1.2 lb. in 1774 and about 1.3 in 1784, an increase complained of. The Special Provision Committee suggested that meat should be cut down to 8 oz. and that a share of potatoes should be issued at the rate of twenty-eight persons to a peck, because the quantity 'for each person exceeds considerably the proportion of what is usually eaten in private families', an improbable statement.[1]

The Shrewsbury House of Industry gave 10½ lb. of bread, nearly 3 lb. of meat and 6 oz. of cheese weekly, the balance being made up in the usual way.[2] At a new workhouse put up at Boldre, Hampshire,

[1] Edward Rigby, *Reports of the Special Committee appointed* . . . (Norwich 1788), p. 26.

[2] L. Wood, *Some Accounts of the Shrewsbury House of Industry* (1795, 4th ed.), p. 102.

just before 1796, an unvarying breakfast of beef broth or milk porridge and bread was served, as was a bread and cheese supper of 6 oz. of bread and 1 oz. of cheese for adults, with less for children, the supper being sometimes varied by potatoes. Dinners were in a weekly series. On Sundays 4 oz. of meat for adults, 3 oz. for children with plenty of vegetables and bread; on Mondays warmed-up Sunday's remains, on Tuesdays 1 lb. of pudding, children ¾ lb., the same on Wednesday Thursday and Friday, and on Saturday the paupers had the satisfaction of making a clearance of all that remained, or, if this was short, bread and cheese.

Much the same sort of routine feeding was observed at Headingley in the West Riding. Here the poor were provided with thick water pottage with milk, beer, or treacle at choice for breakfast and supper, an exhilarating diet no doubt. Sunday's dinner was ½ lb. of boiled beef or mutton with bread and vegetables, and, crowning mercy, broth; Mondays, cold meat, potatoes, bread and 1 pint of beer; Tuesdays, puddings of fine flour, bread and 1 pint of beer; Wednesday, Thursday and Friday, the same; Saturday, drink pottage, bread and a pint. In an unidentified East Riding House about 1780 much the same food was issued.

The Nacton, Norfolk, House of Industry gave bread and cheese, butter and milk always for supper and for Sunday breakfast in 1773. Other breakfasts were milk or beef broth. Dinner was beef and dumplings on three days, but baked suet pudding on Monday, rice milk or broth on Wednesday, and bread and butter on Friday and Saturday, kept the expense low. Instead of the bread and butter dinners, pease porridge was formerly served, but the diners preferred bread and butter because they had tea with it, and it was said that they were supplied with the best quality of food, no neighbouring poor living near so well in their own cottages and not one little farmer in ten. The food in debtors' and criminal prisons was on a more meagre scale.

The mainstay of the workhouse diet was bread and cheese, butter being eaten with it for breakfast and supper, or some kind of mess of pottage. Meat varied, but if it was served three times a week, the poor were luckier than those of independent life; and the balance of the days was filled in with more bread, or some cheap cereal substitute, or broth. Contemporary statements that inmates were better fed than their social equals outside are confirmed by labourers' budgets of the time.

Besides actual budgets there are three contemporary estimates by persons of some experience which are a guide to then informed opinion. William Pitt of Pendeford, Staffordshire, was a regular contributor to the *Annals of Agriculture*, the compiler of his county report and a writer on farming for other periodicals. He says that 1 lb. of meat a week *per capita* of the whole population, including children, was a liberal allowance. The annual expense of a family, man, wife and four children, included bread corn at 5 lb. each, the produce of a cow in milk, butter and cheese, twelve slices of pork or bacon, slightly less than 5 lb. a week for the family and 6 lb. of butcher's meat a week. The produce, in beer, of 24 lb. of malt is also allowed. This estimate is not intended to represent the economy of a family of the lower classes, who could never expect to obtain such liberal diet, but an average allowance taking in rich and poor.

The budget of a childless labourer and his wife recorded by the Rev. James Willis, of Sopley, Hampshire, in 1808, supports Pitt. No fresh meat or beer is included. Two gallons of bread or flour, 1 lb. of salt, 2 lb. of bacon, 1 lb. each of butter and cheese weekly and 6 lb. of tea annually completes the statement of their regimen. 'This is,' states the Reverend, 'in general a correct statement of the condition of the poor throughout the kingdom,' and goes on to prove that they could not buy even that without parish aid.

Of Bedford, that year, Thomas Batchelor wrote: 'Most of the farmers that are not very poor are in the habit of purchasing some joint of meat for the Sabbath day at least,' and the common diet of this class included 2 lb. of salted pork, 1 lb. of cheese, ½ lb. of butter, ⅓ lb. of sugar, 1 oz. of tea weekly, and 1 lb. 4 oz. of brown bread or common pudding, one-third of a gallon of skimmed milk, 1½ pints of small beer and 1 pint of ale daily, so that the Hampshire labourer's diet was an improvement on that of the Bedfordshire farmer in the allowance of meat, milk and ale as well as butter and cheese. The board given to servants in this county was not very generous. Men got a mess of milk, made by crumbling bread into it, or boiled milk only for breakfast and supper, and in addition bread and cheese and occasionally meat.

The collection of actual budgets of labourers in husbandry was undertaken by three enthusiasts, Eden, Davies and the Rev. Arthur Young of Sussex, the renowned Arthur's son. The arrangement of the heads of expenditure given by all are about the same and this is probably as much the result of uniform diet as of deliberate intention on the investigator's part. The first two cover practically the whole country; Young confines himself to the neighbourhood of Glynde, Sussex.

The list of necessities is set out: bread, flour or oatmeal; yeast and salt; thread and worsted; bacon or other meat; tea, sugar and butter; soap; candles; cheese, beer; potatoes. The quantities bought are not given and only in some examples are sufficiently detailed commodity prices attached to enable the quantities to be calculated. Naturally the amounts spent on the different items vary with the choice and necessities of the individual and with the amount earned. Much the largest sum is spent on bread, flour or oatmeal and the composition of the bread is different in different parts of the country. Where the family is larger the proportion of the weekly expenditure on bread rises, and generally higher wages or a smaller family means more spent on meat. This item varies from none at all to 1 lb. or more a week, rising occasionally to 6 or 7 lb. a week for the family. Cheese is not a heavy item and very little beer is drunk, usually not a pint a head a week. Potatoes are eaten in varying quantities, but these are not large and their consumption depends to some extent on the district, as in Sussex—

> All among the rooks and crows
> Where the good potatoes grows;

or in Lancashire and further north. Small quantities of tea, sugar and butter find their way to the larder. These statements are undoubtedly representative of the country as a whole, because Eden and Davies cover twenty-two counties and Young's Sussex adds one more.

Compared with this, two estimates for the earlier part of the century, 1737 and 1777, prepared by a pamphleteer, the author of *Reasons for the late increase in the Poor-Rates*, 1777, are rather generous. They purport to be averages for the whole country and cover a family of man, wife and four small children. At both dates the weekly estimates include 43 lb. of bread, 10 lb. of beef or mutton, 4 lb. of cheese *or* 2 lb. of butter and 24 pints of small beer. There is one significant reduction. In 1737 24 pints of milk are allowed weekly; in 1777 only eighteen, a considerable reduction in nutrient value. The writer claims that he does not exaggerate and makes the pertinent observation: 'How much worse off are larger families, who live on bread and water, "a gaol allowance".'

This general description can be expanded here only by a succinct account of the differences in bread-stuffs and other articles of food in different parts of the country.

Eden was in no doubt as to the usual diet in the Weald of Kent. It was bread, milk, potatoes, tea and cheese: little or no meat was used; very little beer and no butter. In spite of this Boys, the county reporter, writing in 1813, is of the opinion that the labourers were often better off than the small farmers of other counties and some small tenants of this. Very few of those who were sober and industrious but had a pork tub to go to for a dinner. Arthur Young, the father, noticed with approbation the diet of the Sussex labourer at about this time. 'The usual breakfast of a labourer, in this part of the world,' he says, 'is broth, made of a coarse ends of beef, with oatmeal flour and butter; or boiled milk; or bread and cheese. His dinner is sometimes pork and bacon. His supper, bread and milk and cheese; new milk half a pint. Good fare.'

Through the south-western counties the diet was less generous, except in Hampshire, which Gilbert White praises. 'The plenty of good wheaten bread,' he says, 'that now is found among all ranks of people in the south, instead of that miserable sort which used in the old days to be made of barley and beans, may contribute not a little to the sweetening of their blood and correcting their juices; for the inhabitants of mountainous districts to this day (1789) are still liable to the itch and other cutaneous disorders from a wretchedness and poverty of diet. . . . Every decent labourer has also his garden, which is half his support, as well as his delight; the common farmers provide plenty of beans, peas and greens, for their hinds to eat with their bacon; and those few that do not are despised for their sordid parsimony, and looked upon as regardless of the welfare of their dependants. Potatoes have prevailed in this little district, by means of premiums, within these twenty years only, and are much esteemed here now by the poor, who would scarce have ventured to taste them in the last reign.' An old Hampshire woman told W. H. Hudson a rather different story in 1902, but that properly belongs in the following section.

Barley bread, skim milk cheese, and potatoes with tea were the staples in Dorset, Wiltshire, Somerset, Devon and Cornwall. Some wheaten bread was used in Dorset; it was often eaten alone, with water as the beverage, but in the main there was no doubt an occasional dish of bacon, some odd vegetables and so on throughout all these counties and it was only the very poorest who were forced to subsist on a purely cereal and potato diet. Pilchards were commonly eaten in Cornwall, and some cider was drunk in all these counties.

For Gloucester, and the counties northwards along the borders of Wales, very little information about differences is available. Potatoes were extensively grown in Salop and doubtless largely eaten, but Plymley, in 1803 thought less bacon was eaten by the labourers then than formerly. The Cheshire labourers are said to have had their dishes of potatoes and bacon or butter and drank whey or buttermilk if they could buy it. Bread was wheat or wheat and barley mixed and oatcake or hasty pudding made with oats was a frequent article of diet. Tea was drunk, beer being 'scarcely accessible' to the labourer. A dish called brewes or browis made of slices of bread with fat poured over them was eaten in this county and in Lancashire, and a harvest dish, fitchet pie made of apples, onions and bacon, was served to the labourers.

Barley bread, made in 12 lb. loaves, was almost the only bread used by the Cumberland peasantry, usually baked at home. Clap bread was made of barley here, but of oats in Westmorland. Oatcake and buttermilk was a common meal in Lancashire. Here goats' flesh, which was cured like bacon, was called 'mountain mutton'. The failure of the potato crop in 1793 made a gloomy outlook, for it was the principal food of the lower classes.

> *In Oldham brewis wet and warm*
> *And Rochdale's puddings there's no harm.*

Arthur Young[1] found that all sorts of cereal mixtures were used in the northern counties when he toured them in 1770, just as they had been in the days of Henry Best. He specifically mentions them at the following places: oatbread, Barnsley; maslin (mixed wheat and rye), Guisborough, Scorton, Kiplin, Swinton, Sleningfold, Aysgarth; rye bread, Raby Castle, from Durham to Newcastle; rye, wheat and pease or barley and pease, Belford, Hetton, Fenton near Wooler and Rothbury, Wallington and Cholford Bridge, the last two using also beans and oatmeal. At High Ascot barley or barley and rye were used and these cereals or mixtures of them, sometimes with wheat, were normal at other places too numerous to list. At Kendal market where very few potatoes were to be seen in 1730, about thirty-five carts of 2,520 stone were sold weekly in 1830.

Northumberland is described in a folk rhyme:

> *Rothbury for goats' milk,*
> *And the Cheviots for mutton,*
> *Cheswick for its cheese and bread,*
> *And Tynemouth for a glutton.*

Yorkshire feeding was much the same as that of the other northern

[1] Arthur Young, *A Six Months' Tour through the N. of England* (1770, 2nd ed.), iii, passim.

counties, with perhaps special emphasis on oats, although some other mixed cereals were used and, near Hull, pure wheaten bread. Oat bread was also very usual in Derby and the moorlands of Stafford, but by 1808 potatoes had come to form a large part of the labourer's diet in Stafford.

Warwick and Leicester labourers used wheaten bread, and in the former county pork or bacon, boiled or broiled and cut in slices was eaten, when it could be got, with an onion on a piece of wheaten bread washed down with water if there was no beer. The labourers were reputed in 1813 to 'have as great respect for beer in this county as in any in England, and if it is possible to procure ale, they will not want it, if their wives and children should go naked'—but on the whole opinion tended to believe that here as in Northampton, where bread of one-third rye, one-third wheat and one-third barley was eaten, the labourer did not fare too badly. Oxford and Berkshire were much the same, occasional meals of bacon being possible, but an Oxford labourer born in 1815 remembered that in the days of his youth the cottager lived on barley bread and potatoes and seldom tasted meat.[1]

The poet, John Clare (1793–1864), who was Northampton born, writes:

> But the beechen bowl, that once supplied
> The feast of frumenty, is thrown aside
> And the old freedom that was living then
> When masters made them merry with their men
> When all their coats alike were russet brown
> And his rude speech was vulgar as their own.

Barley bread had probably given place to wheat in Buckinghamshire by the end of the eighteenth century, and in Bedfordshire wheat had almost entirely superseded maslin by that date, although in one of the workhouses oatmeal was used. The Eastern Counties also had turned to wheat, and potatoes in Essex were praised by Arthur Young. They were unknown in 1767, but he thought that their increased consumption had made up to the poor for the rise in price of meat, butter, cheese, etc., since that date.

The general impression from all the evidence is that the labourers and smaller farmers lived generally on a monotonous, even inadequate diet, mainly of bread with cheese, butter and milk if they were lucky, and bread and water or stewed tea when they were not. They may

[1] Most of this information is drawn from the County Reports already referred to.

have had a small weekly allowance of meat, usually bacon. Only in the central, eastern and south-eastern counties was the wheaten loaf the regular food of this class and in this district there were exceptions to the rule. The whole of the country from Dorset south-westward, the Marcher counties and the North were in the habit of using the so-called inferior cereals or maslin. Most of these parts were able to obtain buttermilk or whey and a great deal of pottage was eaten. This was probably not a bad sort of food and when it was supplemented by vegetables, and in the later years of the century by potatoes, was fairly efficient, although the diet of the time undoubtedly had an effect on the incidence of disease. It is, however, clear that less milk was drunk in the rural districts as the century advanced, especially in the south where it was not possible for the cottager to keep a cow, and the substitution of milk by potatoes, which seems to have been the tendency, certainly caused a lack of balance.

The monotony of the average countryman's diet was broken by feasting at the harvest, and at other times such as Christmas. Special arrangements were, however, sometimes made against the extra cost of harvest food. William Ellis says that old ewes and wethers were picked out and put into the clover so that they would be fat for 'mutton pyes' for the reapers, a crone ewe making 'harvest beef'.

It is by no means clear that there was a marked change either way in the cottager's diet during the century. If anything, there must have been some depression towards 1800, but on the whole the poorer rural classes lived on very much the same sort of food for at least the past 200 years, if not much longer. The spread of the wheaten loaf is more marked in the Victorian age, until its use became general owing to the development of modern conditions. Even in 1838 the old ways of living had not disappeared from the remoter country districts, as William Howitt found, where the habit or necessity of eating meat only once a week was usual, and there were thousands of people in Lancashire, Yorkshire, Cumberland and the Peak of Derbyshire who would not thank you for wheaten bread. This was true much later, and the same conditions that Cowper described—

> . . . and the brown loaf
> Lodged on the shelf, half eaten without sauce
> Of savoury cheese, or butter costlier still—

went on far into the Victorian era.

PART THREE

THE VICTORIAN AGE (1837–1901)

NOTABLE EVENTS

Age of Reform, 1832–67. Repeal of the Combination Acts, 1824. Beginnings of modern trade unionism in the late 1840's. First Factory Act, 1833. London and Manchester Railway, 1830. New Poor Law, 1834. National education, 1834. The Chartists, 1839–48. Repeal of the Corn Laws, 1846. First Trade Union Congress, 1868. Education Act, 1870.

Population of England
1821, 13 million. 1871, 22¾ million. 1901, 36 million. 1931, 40 million.

VIII INTRODUCTORY

THE New Poor Law was passed in 1834, and marks a definite change in the position of the cottager. Queen Victoria came to the throne in 1837; the Royal Agricultural Society of England was founded in 1839 to take the place of the semi-official Board of Agriculture the Government of the day had allowed to expire a decade before.

The position of the farm labourer had indeed become so serious that it was time that something was done to improve it. Nobody was in any doubt about his evil condition, and many were exercised about it. It had indeed become somewhat the fashion to look back to supposedly better days, and Cobbett was not the least of those who did so.

In *Twopenny Trash* (1831) he writes with a fine glow of indignation: 'All of you who are 60 years of age can recollect that bread and meat and not wretched potatoes were the food of the labouring people; you can recollect that every industrious labouring man brewed his own beer and drank it by his own fireside; . . . you can recollect when the young people were able to provide money before they were married to purchase decent furniture for a house, and had no need to go to the parish to furnish them with a miserable nest to creep into; you can recollect when a bastard child was a rarity in a village . . . when every sober and industrious labourer had his Sunday coat . . . when a young man was pointed at if he had not on a Sunday a decent coat upon his back, a good hat upon his head, a clean shirt with silk handkerchief round his neck, leather breeches without a spot, whole worsted stockings tied under the knee with a red garter, a pair of handsome Sunday shoes . . . (with) silver buckles.'

Similar language was used by Thomas Postans.[1] 'Thirty-five years

[1] Thomas Postans, *A Letter to Sir Thomas Baring, Bt., M.P.* (1831).

ago the Agricultural Labourer possessed a home to shelter him, a family to comfort him and food to sustain him. In most cases he was either a resident on the farm where he laboured, or lived in a cottage in a neighbouring village. Where he was without the reach of coal, he gathered wood, furze or turf with little or no molestation . . . his garden was indeed small and ill cultivated. The value of potatoes was neither so well known or so highly appreciated as it is at present; and the idea of subsiding upon potatoes alone, as an article of food, was not entertained by the labourer of England. Bread was made at home, which, though coarser than that in present use, was not on that account less nourishing food for the labouring man. In times of distress bread and water sustained him at his last extremity.'

Both exaggerate the prosperity of the labourer in an earlier day, but that is a foible of human beings. Informed opinion had held for a century that a large proportion of the agricultural wages·paid did not cover the cost of subsistence and was helped out by poor relief. The effect of the economic developments of the second half of the eighteenth century was to increase this necessity and Gilbert's Act of 1782 excluded the able-bodied paupers from the parochial workhouse, ordering work to be found for them at or near their homes. This was followed by the Act of 1795 which sanctioned relief at home, or, as it has come to be called, outdoor relief. In May of 1795 the Berkshire Justices had anticipated this Act by their system of regulating relief by the price of bread This system, which became known as the Speenhamland system, granted assistance in accordance with the number of a man's family to a settled bread scale. Wages were supplemented by parish pay to bring them up to the required standard and where there were no wages the parish was obliged to find the whole amount. The labourers were sent round the farmers in the parish to seek employment, and when they got it, the farmer, who knew the supplement was forthcoming, did not pay economic wages, although he must have known that he would have to pay his share of the balance in the form of Poor Rates. The subject is complex, and has been fully discussed in a number of works, notably by J. L. and Barbara Hammond, *The Village Labourer*, so it is unnecessary to develop it here *in extenso*.

Besides doles, other suggestions were put forward towards the amelioration of the difficult lot of the labourer. Among these food reform figured prominently, but the labourers steadfastly refused to accept these suggestions, for the very excellent reasons given by the Hammonds. The reformers did not realize that 'a romantic and adventurous appetite is one of the blessings of an easy life and that the more miserable a man's condition, and the fewer his comforts, the more does he shrink from experiments in diet'.

Whitbread's attempts to introduce legislation calling for a minimum wage were a more practical attack on the problem, but were defeated by a government which believed only too completely in the doctrines of *laissez faire*. It was considered preferable to maintain the agricultural labourer on a minimum subsistence by a supplement to his wages from the poor rates, and for forty years from the Act of 1795 to 1834 this was done. In the Hammond's words 'The Poor Law, which had once been the hospital, became now the prison of the poor. Designed to relieve his necessities, it was now his bondage. If a labourer was in private employment, the difference between the wage his master chose to give and the recognized minimum was made up by the parish. Those labourers who could not find private employment were either shared out among the ratepayers or else their labour was sold by the parish to employers at a low rate, the parish contributing what was needed to bring the labourer's receipts up to scale. Crabbe has described the roundsman system—

> *Alternate masters now their Slave command*
> *Urge the weak efforts of his feeble hand,*
> *And when his age attempts its task in vain,*
> *With ruthless taunts, of lazy poor complain.*

'The meshes of the Poor Law were spread over the entire labour system. The labourers, stripped of their ancient rights and their ancient possessions, refused a minimum wage and allotments, were given instead a universal system of pauperism. This was the basis on which the governing class rebuilt the English village. Many critics, Arthur Young and Malthus among them, assailed it, but it endured for forty years, and it was not disestablished until Parliament itself had passed through a revolution,' meaning the Reform Act of 1832.

The forty years during which these Israelites wandered in the wilderness stretched from the Act of 1795, which confirmed the scale allowance system, until the Poor Law Reform Act of 1834. Russell M. Garnier's words describe their situation poignantly. He wrote *The Annals of the British Peasantry* (1895), and of this time says: 'As soon as the scale allowance system was adopted in any parish, all fared alike, whether industrious or idle, and a struggle commenced among the occupiers which had for its primary object the equal distribution of

H

the rate on the labourer. In some parishes the whole of this class was paid from the poor rate; in others after a certain portion of it—according to the acreage—had been distributed among the occupiers by mutual consent, the remainder was paid out of the rates. The men thus receiving "scale pay" were employed as roundsmen, or allotted to the occupiers according to the extent of each occupation. Acre by acre, a whole administrative centre became in this way a convict colony. Family by family, its entire labouring population degenerated into paupers, bound to toil, but labouring, as it was pointed out, "with the reluctance of slaves and the turbulence of demoralized freemen for their bankrupt master, the parish" . . . the occupiers were careful not to detect cases of malingering . . . and thus placed a premium on imposture. . . . The paupers regarded this payment (the parish) as a right and called it their income. . . . The allowance of gallon loaves was termed by each recipient his "bread" or "make-up" money.'

The scale allowance applied to children as well as adults and the labourer got the equivalent of so many loaves or the loaves themselves for each child. A bright spot in the administration of the system was its all-inclusiveness. No one was omitted and it was in some sort an advantage to have children for whom the allowance could be drawn. No enquiry was made into the state of wedlock of the parents and many single women drew allowances for one, two and three children. They were considered fortunate, and, of course, such a system, to rate it low, did nothing to discourage a deal of casual and irresponsible sexual indulgence. Lord Ernle (English Farming Past and Present), who thought the worst effects of the system did not make themselves felt until 1813, because there had been some rise in monetary wages, quotes W. Jacob (1817) as authority for the statement that a great part of the farm labourers were then absolutely destitute apart from the scale allowance, which put a premium on recklessness in marriage and out of it. A Swaffham woman, for instance, who had five illegitimate children to support, got 18s. a week, much more than any individual labourer could earn. The cost of pauperism per head, in 1832, was about 15s. a year.

Fortunately not every parish adopted the roundsman system, and some labourers also resented the system, while as time went on some farmers would not resist the obvious conclusion that this cheap labour, as it seemed, was really very dear in fact. A few parishes refused relief to able-bodied paupers except in well regulated workhouses, and a larger number made hard work at low pay a condition of parish relief.

These were the circumstances that begot a poem on 'Poverty' by
·Thomas Shoel, a Somerset labourer, poet and musician of the late
eighteenth and early nineteenth century, mentioned by Llewellyn
Powys in his *Somerset Essays* (1937). It runs—

> *Begin with him who with such constant toil*
> *Ploughs up the field and cultivates the soil*
>
> *Then homeward see him labour on his way,*
> *And close the toil of long and tedious day;*
> *His poor coarse meal then soon behold him take*
> *Potatoes salted, or a barley cake;*
> *Cold water serves his painful thirst to slake,*
> *Or Indian leaves a half strained beverage make:*
> *His lisping prattlers hang on either knee,*
> *Well pleas'd again their father's face to see;*
>
> *His dear lov'd partner eyes him with delight,*
> *So well beloved, so pleasing in her sight*
> *And both perhaps let fall the trickling tear,*
> *While they behold in rags their children dear.*
>
> *Whose scanty meal soon finished see him hie*
> *On clotted flocks or beds of dust to lie,*
> *Whose santy head and foot can scarce contain*
> *Himself, his partner and his hapless train*

And it was between 1820 and 1830 that the rumbustious Cobbett
performed his *Rural Rides* and poured out the vials of his wrath on those
whom he supposed to be responsible for the deplorable state in which
all the partners of the farming industry then found themselves. The
weight of the depression, however, clearly pressed most heavily on
the labourers, and Cobbett was never at a loss to condemn those who
allowed this to be so. He demands that their conditions be looked at.
Of Knighton in Leicestershire he declaims, 'Look at these hovels, made
of mud and straw: bits of glass or of old cast-off windows, without
frames or hinges frequently. Enter them and look at the bits of chairs
and stools; the wretched boards tacked together to form a table; the
floor of pebble, broken brick, or of the bare ground; look at the thing
called a bed; and survey the rags on the backs of the wretched
inhabitants',

People who had lived on the diet and under the general economic conditions of the farm workers from 1796 to 1830 were hardly likely to be sturdy and energetic workers—making every possible allowance for the variation in conditions indicated above. And it is a somewhat curious thing that once the drastic surgery of the New Poor Law, 1834, was applied the farmers themselves realized the fact. At any time in the previous twenty years they would have declared that they could not provide full employment, at any rate if they had to pay all the necessary weekly wage, for all the available labour, but almost immediately the Act forbidding outdoor relief had been passed they began to absorb it. So soon as 1837, the year of Queen Victoria's accession, a Sussex farmer told a Commons' Committee that the thirty or forty men who had to be provided with work, or even paid without working, had nearly all found employment in the parish. Three or four had gone to sea. The farmers had also begun to find jobs for wet weather, when the men had invariably been turned away. And the Lords' Committee on the State of Agriculture was told, in 1836, that in Hampshire the unemployed had all been absorbed locally; more men would indeed have been useful. Other counties were not so fortunate, and the children who had drawn the bread allowance now had to go to work on the farms to do their minute share towards closing the gap between wages and the cost of living on a scale that would be intolerable to-day.

The industry as a whole was, however, by 1836 beginning slowly to recover from the post-war depression and the effects of speculation outside its own doors, and the period 1840–80, with the exception of the last two years, was on the whole one of prosperity for the farmer and his landlord. One result was the formation of the Agricultural Society of England in 1839; it soon became the 'Royal', and took the place of the Board of Agriculture which had died of inanition more than anything else in 1819. Among many other things the 'Royal' took an interest in the condition of the labourer and many essays on that subject, on designs for cottages, on education, and so on, appeared in the pages of its journal. Some of these were by people who had actually carried out on their own estates the reforms they recommended to other people: some were theorists, but usually theorists who had a knowledge of their subject. More provincial societies, like the 'Bath and West' and the Yorkshire Agricultural Society agitated the same questions.

Lord Shaftesbury's agitation about the conditions of employment and living in the new factory towns, too, had some effect in stirring up interest in the condition of the farm labourers. Industrialists were only too ready to reply to his accusations by pointing out that very much the same conditions applied in some rural areas. As a consequence there were many Royal Commissions appointed to examine the labourer's circumstances and to suggest a remedy, if remedy was needed. All these provide some indications of the farm worker's way of living and can be supplemented by the writings of private philanthropists and reformers.

IX COTTAGES

THE picturesque continued to occupy those concerned with the theory of cottages until at least 1870. Traces of it can still be found in newly built, suburban dormitory villages to-day; but the theory of cottages also engaged the attention of philanthropic landowners up to the debacle of 1879, when farms and farm buildings and lastly farm cottages practically ceased to be rebuilt, and often were not even repaired for some thirty years. The facts of rural housing engaged many private persons and public bodies, and the numerous Royal Commissions appointed during the nineteenth century whose terms of reference concerned farming and the farm worker. What were the theories and what effect had they on the reality?

Halévy accuses the farmer of 1815 of lack of humanity. He saw no need for the elegant cottages built pretentiously in Gothic, like those to be seen on the estates of some great landowners. A mud hovel, dark and badly ventilated was quite sufficient. There must be no field to take up some of the labourer's time. A tiny kitchen garden was enough, with room to keep a pig, but not grazing enough for a cow. This is a dark saying and can hardly have been universally applicable, though rather less than an uncommon outlook.

Already by 1830 Thomas Postans was suggesting that it was necessary to rebuild many of the farm cottages and to allow half an acre of land to each. The frontispiece to his pamphlet shows a pair of cottages with a living room 14 ft. by 13 ft. and two bedrooms 10 ft. by 9 ft. on the ground floor and two pantries or other store rooms. There was a shed at the back and a pigsty beyond that. They were to have clay and straw walls and pole and thatch roofs and could be built for £35 a pair, the proposed rent being £3 or £4 a year, not a bad return on the money. The accommodation was by no means generous, but it was nearly equal to that planned by the Rev. Copinger Hill[1] thirteen years later,

[1] Rev. Copinger Hill in *Journal of R. Agric. Soc.* (1843), p. 356 *et seq.*

who did, however, put his two bedrooms upstairs. What he thought
necessary was a living room about 13 ft. square, a pantry or cellar about
8 ft. by 13 ft. including stairs with a closet under and two bedrooms
over these. The height should be 8 ft. below, 6 ft. 4 in. above stairs.
A bedroom on the ground floor was not desirable. About a quarter of
an acre of garden was to be attached to these dwellings of stone 14 in.
thick or clay with a thatched or reed roof.

George Nicholls,[1] three years later, thought that the larger amount
of capital then needed for a farm enterprise as well as other factors
had tended to increase the distance between the farmer and the labourer,
a process that had been in progress for 300 years. No cottage ought in
his opinion to have less than four rooms, two up and two down, and
the ground floor ought to be raised 18 in. above the ground level,
suitably drained; one bedroom should have a fire-place. He did not
think the building materials mattered so long as the home was roomy
and comfortable. There should be a garden.

The Duke of Bedford, who had been building improved cottages
on his Bedford and Devon estates having one, two or three bedrooms
as necessary, described them for the 'Royal' in 1849 and passed the somewhat cynical comment that landlords 'while they are building and
improving farmhouses, homesteads and cattle sheds, (should) also
build and improve dwellings for their labourers'. J. Young McVicar
in the same year drew nearer to modern ideas with plans with a porch
up two steps giving separate access to a scullery 9 ft. 6 in. by 9 ft.,
with a boiler and sink and a living room 14 ft. by 13 ft., a pantry 8 ft.
by 6 ft. and a closet under the stairs and three bedrooms 14 ft. by 10 ft.,
9 ft. 6 in. by 9 ft. and 9 ft. by 8 ft. In addition a coalhouse, privy and
dustbin are provided. A second set of plans details slightly larger rooms.

John C. Morton, whose *Cyclopædia of Agriculture* first appeared in
1856, said that cottages could be built in one or two storeys, the second
type being used as two dwellings, an original thought: but the two-
storey individual dwelling was 'preferable in economy, convenience
and healthfulness'. Even his single storey plans provide three bedrooms, but two of them are very small. He proposes a water closet
and suggests that a bed can be put in a recess in the living room (12 ft.
by 12 ft.) if necessary. One two-storey plan has only two upstairs
bedrooms, the other three. All are to have water closets and a cesspool,
open fires and windows to open.

[1] George Nicholls in ibid., iii, p. 17.

A late example of the picturesque is to be found in the 2nd edition (1870) of C. J. Richardson's *The Englishman's House*, which provides plans and elevations of gardeners' and other cottages stated to have been erected on estates. There is little exceptional about these plans, which are possibly more than usually ornate. Only a year later John Dent confessed in the 'Royal' Journal that 'in the matter of cottages we have still much to accomplish'—a masterly understatement, and in 1872 the plans submitted for the prizes offered by the Marquis of Bath and Major Picton Turberville were not good enough for the judges to make the awards. The next year, however, they improved the plans submitted by 'Rusticus' to the following standard: an entrance passage with pantry and stairs on one side, closet under stairs, pump indoors, shed and coalhouse at back: living room 11 ft. 6 in. by 13 ft. 6 in., scullery 10 ft. by 8 ft., three bedrooms 11 ft. 6 in. by 12 ft., 8 ft. 6 in. by 8 ft. 6 in. and 10 ft. by 8 ft. They were to be built in pairs. This, with the addition of a parlour and the usual urban amenities of main drainage, water supply, gas and electricity, is almost as adequate as many thousands of suburban houses which were put up in dormitory areas of the great cities between 1918 and 1938. It is an ideal that could only be amplified in the size and height of rooms and in fact remained roughly the ideal until and including the *Report of the Advisory Committee on Rural Cottages* (1914).

Many ancient cottages are still inhabited, improved here and there, and it remains to estimate what progress was made during the reign of Queen Victoria to bring cottages up to this very modest standard. For this purpose there is available a number of authoritative modern historical works which include this subject among more general matter, and they take, necessarily, their evidence from the reports of the various Royal Commissions, beginning with that on *The Employment of Women and Children in Agriculture* of 1843 and from the writings of contemporaries, such as Richard Heath, the Revd. Augustus Jessopp and others. To these may be added some dozens of more modern descriptive writers and editors of living farm-workers' reminiscences—a popular form of publication in the past half century—which often contain relevant information as a kind of by-blow.

Reference has already been made to the one-room dwellings of Northumberland, where in Glendale at any rate, the great John Grey of Dilston and his contemporaries had made rich and successful farming land out of a wilderness, and a county where Cobbett had been astonished by the size and apparent prosperity of the farms. Near

Alnwick 'the labourers live in a sort of *barracks*; that is to say, long sheds with stone walls and covered with what are called pantiles. They have neither gardens, nor privies, nor backdoors. . . . There are no villages, no scattered cottages; no upstairs; one little window and one doorway to each dwelling in the shed or barrack'. Each section was about 17 ft. by 15 ft., no ceiling, the earth the floor. The man, wife and family all lived in this one room. This was strange to Cobbett,[1] but the one room and double-ended house had been a commonplace of that district time out of mind. At the opposite end of the country, on Exmoor, similar long buildings like a shed sometimes contained two or three farmhouses, and Samuel Sidney provides a picture of them in his essay on *Exmoor Reclamation* in the Royal Journal, 1878.

On the Greenwich Hospital estates in Northumberland, John Grey of Dilston, writing in the same Journal for 1844, reports that cottages of a rather more ample kind had been built of freestone with a living room 22 ft. 6 in. by 15 ft. and a bedroom over, with a lean-to 6 ft. wide at the side. Earl Grey was perhaps more generous at Howick, having provided a living room 15 ft. or 16 ft. by 16 ft., coal pantry and pigsty and one or two bedrooms above—the description is not quite clear, but the one-roomed dwelling continued in use until quite modern times. Caird remarked it with repugnance in 1851. The Report on the Sanitary Conditions of the Labouring Population of England for 1842 mentions their leaky walls and wet clay floors. They were described almost in Cobbett's words by a Royal Commission in 1867, although in Glendale (John Grey's district) and elsewhere in the county, the landowner's agents were getting alive to the necessity, and better cottages were being built 'everywhere'. Richard Heath (*The English Peasant*) found the one-room cottage 'often' in 1872, and the Royal Commission on Labour of 1893 states that the two-end houses were preferred by the labourers. The same old description is given. One room 16 ft. by 21 ft., used as kitchen and sleeping room, and one other smaller room, a small pantry or back kitchen, doubtless the lean-to referred to by earlier writers and a loft above reached by a ladder and often used as a sleeping apartment. The Earl of Tankerville at Chillingham had then recently converted some double-ended cottages into two-storey with two or three good bedrooms upstairs, closets and other refinements, but no idea of how many had been converted in this way is given.

[1] William Cobbett, *Rural Rides* (1893), ii, pp. 378, 386.

The limitations imposed by the kind of descriptive writing on which reliance must be placed for the history of the nineteenth century, form the great difficulty in estimating the progress made in Victorian times. Terms like 'many bad, some good' occur with amazing frequency in the reports, and the greater and more explicit details given by some refer only to limited areas. So far as Northumberland is concerned, for example, the number of cottages which had been built by, say, 1837 is not known, and although there is some information in the Census about the number of farm workers, no one can now discover what accommodation existing cottages provided for them, and in the absence of any evidence of how many good cottages were built, how many bad ones improved and so on, any accurate estimate of developments is impossible. There is thus great danger of thinking that the conditions were (by modern urban standards) intolerably bad or that they were being rapidly and adequately improved—according to the colour of one's mind; and this is no less true of other counties as well.

Another district reclaimed a little later than Glendale was the Lincoln Heath and Wolds. This large area was mainly brought into cultivation in the early nineteenth century. When this work was done a great farmhouse was often built in the midst of the former waste 'like a settlement in a primeval forest'. It had no cottages for labourers attached to it and occasionally the few cottages that had existed were pulled down, the settlement of day labourers being opposed. The labour employed consisted of farm servants living-in, supplemented by children, young persons and women, the first of the 'gangs' whose employment was later regulated by legislation. Here it is obvious that new cottages would eventually be required, because the population was bound to increase with the intensification of farming methods. The Royal Commission on the Employment of Children etc. (1867) reported that there was an outcry for more and better cottages, especially since the passing of the Union Chargeability Act of 1865. Then the old cottages were of 'mud and stud', two storeys high, the upper being open to the roof and sometimes without any window. Two 'or more generally one bedroom sufficed'. In some eight parishes there were twenty-five cottages with three bedrooms, 193 with two, 178 with one. Lord Yarborough and the late Mr. Heneage had anticipated the demand by building new cottages, no details of which are provided, but on some few large properties there was hardly any improvement. Much the same conditions obtained in 1893 round Louth and Holbeach. Cottages were kept in good repair on the great estates, but were poorly

looked after by small-scale owners. The new ones had two or three
rooms down, one being a scullery, and three above. Of the old,
nineteen-twentieths of the whole were two up and two down. The
best rooms in these were 10 ft. to 14 ft. square. The back bedroom
often had a roof sloping to within 3 ft. or 4 ft. of the floor. Access to
the upper floor by a ladder was still common in some villages, and
where there was any drainage at all it was by drains to a common
cesspool which overflowed into the ditch. Some people threw their
slops on to the gardens. The water supply was generally ample, one well
to each block of cottages, but there was often only one privy to two or
three houses. There were gardens and allotments, and potato ground
was often supplied (this means ploughed, etc., by the farmer), especially
in the Wolds, and pigs were usually kept, a mark of some measure of
good conditions.

In the other northern counties many eighteenth-century cottages,
of course, continued to be occupied in the nineteenth, but there was
some building on the great estates. In Holderness the Report of 1867
indicates that most of the cottages were four roomed, two up and
two down. On the Wolds at Bishop Burton there was one large room
15 ft. by 13 ft. by 10 ft. high below and two bedrooms, and some slight
variations on this theme in other villages, but only in the Vale of
York and in Howden had three bedrooms made their appearance.
Conditions in the West Riding varied greatly from one down and
one up at Monk Frystone to two, three and four rooms at Airmin,
but few cottages in the three Ridings had the ideal three bedroom
accommodation. The Rev. J. C. Atkinson (*Forty Years in a Moorland
Parish*, 1891) is emphatic about the bad conditions he found at Danby,
Cleveland, in 1870. He saw two old cruk houses being demolished
about 1885. They had the customary single room, the floor sunk
below the ground level, about 18 ft. square, and a woman who had
lived in one so recently as twenty years before told him, 'Ay, there was
not much room for fancy there'—fancy meaning the simplest dictates
of decency. Perhaps one might add decency as understood by a mid-
Victorian middle class cleric. These buildings had been put up or
extended in 1656. This was a bad example perhaps, but the Report of
1893 tells pretty much the same story as that of 1867, although it
mentions that some cottages with three bedrooms had by then been
put up by Sir Tatton Sykes at Sledmere on the Wolds, and at Easing-
wold water supply and drainage were then being engineered. At
Bilton, in the West Riding, there were still many cottages with only

two rooms, but some had two down and three up. Drainage arrangements were as varied as the accommodation. Some villages had waterworks, but most 'inadequate arrangements'. Some of the drains ran into becks and some into cesspools.

The same divergences occurred at Wigton in Cumberland. The cottages farthest north were the worst, being small and low and having no closets or outhouses, but on the Howard and Lonsdale estates good ones with three bedrooms upstairs had been built by 1893. The drainage was often too near the houses, and wells often too near manure heaps. It is characteristic and comprehensible that details of bad cottages only are given, those with one or two rooms only on the ground floor: after all the Assistant Commissioners were looking for bad conditions which needed reforming. In Lancashire, at Garstang, things were much the same. The old cottages were still occupied, but the Earl of Derby and other large landowners had put up some good ones with a living room, kitchen, three bedrooms, a pantry and closet and 14 poles of garden: the general remark is that cottages varied from one room to five or six.

The wide belt across England from East Anglia, Norfolk, Suffolk and Essex to Gloucester and the counties south and south-west of this area, had been the most thickly populated part of the country before the nineteenth century, if a population only so many as about 4½ million in 1600 and about ten million in 1800, when new areas of town were growing in the northern counties, could be said to be dense when spread over such an area. Naturally there were a great many old cottages in this part of the country that did not conform to the ideal of at least five rooms, three of them bedrooms, and it is to the bad examples to which attention is most generally drawn by the Victorian investigators. Even Hasbach, whose *History of the English Agricultural Labourer* is written in a tone of indignation, admits, what is generally already apparent, that the greatest landlords in some counties had built better dwellings, viz.: in Bedford, Stafford, Norfolk, Suffolk and Lincoln, but these model dwellings did not and could not pay an adequate rent, so other investors became frightened of cottage building. The facts were recognized. There were many, most likely a majority, of cottages where the accommodation was insufficient for a very ordinary family, whose roofs were leaky, floors often rotten and full of holes, when not the bare ground or brick or stone laid upon it. By 1889 'no result of sufficient improvement to claim a place in our history' had yet appeared.

Various influences bore upon the progress of improved cottage building. The Union Chargeability Act of 1865 abolished the reasons for the close parish, where cottages were allowed to decay or were pulled down, and a period of good prices and high farming led to some increase in the provision of good cottages by the great estates. The disastrous 70's, culminating in the year 1879, when all crops failed, and all kinds of livestock, cattle and sheep alike, died in their thousands, put an end for twenty years or more to any general prosperity for the farming industry, likewise put a stopper on cottage building, as indeed it did to farmhouse building and maintenance work generally.

The Dukes of Bedford had been among the first great landowners to build good new cottages, but until 1893 these continued to be of three types, with one, two and three bedrooms respectively. The theory was that the one bedroom type was suitable for aged men and or women who had no family, or elderly married couples whose families were grown-up and independent. This was satisfactory where the estate had control of the lettings, but otherwise there was little guarantee that such buildings would not be taken by families simply because there was nothing else available. Outside the Bedford estates in that county, and in Buckinghamshire, George Culley reported in 1867 that in twenty-one villages there were many bad cottages, 'some quite unfit for human beings to live in', and he condemns the village of Ivinghoe as the 'most extraordinary collection of dwellings I ever saw'. Chapman, reporting on St. Neots, in Huntingdon, and Bedford in 1893, states once again that the new cottages on estates were the best, the Duke of Manchester having built some nice ones at Graffham with a living room 12 ft. by 14 ft., a kitchen and three nice bedrooms. But at Eynesbury, St. Neots and Little Stoughton there were some very bad ones, with occasionally only two rooms, one above the other. The whole district had a poor water supply, mainly from shallow, probably surface, wells.

The Union of Swaffham in Norfolk was divided into two districts in 1867: one of eighteen parishes, the other fifteen. Some 4,136 persons lived in the eighteen parishes, and of the 995 cottages, 255 had one bedroom only, 583 two, and 157 three bedrooms. The other district housed 4,151 cottagers in 1,101 cottages, of which 261 had one bedroom, 694 two and 146 the ideal three. While by any standard a one bedroom cottage could not be thought right and proper for a family, especially when there were adolescent or adult children living at home, L. Marion Springall's warning (*Labouring Life in Norfolk Villages, 1834–1914*) may be repeated here. Village welfare in the nineteenth century must not be judged by present day urban standards. The Board of Guardians, the sanitary authorities, were property owners, and were chary of providing refinements for people who were probably unaware of their absence and who hardly wished for them. Coke of Norfolk, like great 'improving' landowners in other counties, had built some specially good cottages, with three bedrooms, with a living room, kitchen and pantry on the ground floor. Elsewhere there were new four-roomed cottages: but the *Norfolk News* of 1863 (quoted by Miss Springall) reports very primitive conditions at Saxlingham, where the cottages were old and dilapidated, and at Corpusty, where the typical cottage had two small, almost dark, bedrooms, with sloping roofs almost to the floor. The state of sanitation was 'as bad as possible', according to C. S. Read in 1858,[1] and a privy was the last thing most landlords thought of providing for their tenants; moreover the water supply was nearly all from surface wells, sometimes indeed from ditches and ponds. Miss Springall reasonably comments that a great many labouring folk must have owed their lives to the fact that the men drank beer and the women and children tea made from boiled water. Most people who were brought into intimate contact with the two-roomed cottage, not always perhaps including the inhabitants, who had grown up amidst the shifts they enforced, heartily condemned them. The Rev. Augustus Jessopp (*Arcady for Better or Worse*, 1887) is one of them. 'Why you may see whole rows of hovels,' he says, 'in no one of which would any farmer of the parish put his horse for a single night—rows of hovels where there are only two rooms, one above, one below. I could point to three of these disgraceful tenements immediately contiguous to one another, in each of which, by a strange coincidence, there were lately a father, mother and seven children all sleeping in a single room. In one case the mother produced an eighth child in the night, her only helper being her daughter, a girl of fourteen, who did her best while the father ran to fetch the mid-wife.'

Frederick Clifford, the *Times* Commissioner, writing on *The Agricultural Lock-out of 1874* (1875), found equally good and bad conditions in Suffolk. At Livermere, 'the two living rooms, and capital pantry downstairs, the three small bedrooms overhead, the wood-house, and the common oven and wash-house built in the rear, are a usual type of the new cottages which are rising in these villages'. At Bunwell, on Crown property, all the cottages had three

[1] C. S. Read in *Journal of R. Agric. Soc.* (1858), pp. 292-3.

bedrooms, with a sitting room and outhouses, and were substantial comfortable dwellings. Of the rest many had only one bedroom, and one woman had put the children in a loft, and slept on the brick floor of the 'downstairs' until the bottom board of the bed fell to pieces from damp. Exning was an example of the mixed village having sixteen to twenty 'decent respectable cottages' built by the squire, with two bedrooms overhead, a comfortable sitting-room downstairs, a nice bit of garden and common offices in the rear including ovens for bread-making: but these were aristocratic mansions compared with some others in the village, seven or eight of which had but one bedroom. Wilson Fox found conditions in both Norfolk and Suffolk little changed in the same places in 1893.

And so it went across the Midland counties of England. Chapman (1893) says the old cottages in Atcham Union, Salop, were then being turned into cow-houses, just as formerly old farmhouses were turned into cottages. The accommodation varied. Many had three bedrooms, but two was the rule, and the second was often very small. Usually by then each cottage had a separate closet, and some villages had a main sewer. The water supply was fair if by gravitation, but the wells were often unsafe, and some distance away. Good gardens were the rule and pigs often kept.

Midway across the country the cottages in the Wantage Union, Berkshire, were generally very bad, often small and with only one bedroom. Lord Wantage's were of a model character. None was being built with less than three bedrooms, the best 15 ft. by 12 ft., the others 8 ft. by 12 ft., and the living room was 15 ft. square by 8 ft. 6 in. high, with a back kitchen. The worst specimens in the county were then to be found at East and West Hannay, Stowell, part of Childrey, Harwell, Denchworth, East Ilsley and Letcombe Bassett. In many the roofs and floors were out of repair, and there was only one bedroom, the door being often only 5 ft. high and the ceiling 5 ft. 6 in. The water supply was generally satisfactory and the drainage improved, but had not reached a standard to meet the reporter's approval.

It was to one of these villages, presumably, that *Alton Locke* went to address the farm workers, in an ancient earthwork at the top of the Berkshire Downs. Kingsley, who placed this incident about 1845, described the village as 'a knot of thatched hovels, all sinking and leaning every way but the right, the windows patched with paper, the doorways stopped with filth, which surrounded a beershop', a picture he did not fail to repeat in *Yeast* 1851. Across the river, near Reading, another writer, Miss Mitford, has given us sketches of Arborfield in an earlier day, and Uffington, in the west of the Vale of White Horse, is celebrated in *Tom Brown's Schooldays*, and the *Scouring of the White Horse*.

At some time during the 1850's a Frenchman, Henri Taine, wrote his *Notes on England* (1861), and describes a village within 20–30 miles of London which was most likely in Surrey, where several cottages were to his idea very poor 'being of clay covered with laths, a thatched roof; the rooms are too low and too narrow, the windows too small, the partitions too thin . . .', but in Sussex a good farmer in the sixties reduced the six cottages he took with the farm to five because one had only two bedrooms and that was against his principles. His daughter, Maude Robinson, adds that when a South Down farm in the Sixties went into milk production, seven more cottages had to be built for the men required for this trade: but not all those responsible in Sussex were so enlightened. Chapman reporting on Thatcham Union in 1893, however, states that then there were not many with less than two bedrooms and he wanted all privies to be made into earth closets. The water supply was, he said, small and poor. Sussex is a county of great landowners, and among these the Duke of Norfolk and Lord Leconfield had both built new good cottages. The former provided a living room 12 ft. by 12 ft., a kitchen or wash-house, some having a large pantry as well as a wood house and three large bedrooms. At North Stoke Lord Leconfield had gilded the lily by supplying four bedrooms, the same sized living room, kitchen and large garden at 1s. 6d. a week: but elsewhere, for example at Pulborough, there were still small old cottages with a living room 10 ft. square by 7 ft. high, a scullery 8 ft. by 4 ft. and bedrooms of the same size: Cootham had some with a living room 11 ft. square by 6 ft. 6 in. high, a lean-to washhouse and small pantry, one bedroom and a makeshift sleeping apartment over the pantry.

John Halsham, writing of *Idlehurst* (1897), a Sussex village's nickname, says 'The old houses . . . have for the most part large rooms, if low; they are nearly all "detached" with tolerable patches of garden; they were built, with their steep roofs of "Horsham slate" and central chimnies to keep out damp and cold. The new cottages, built by speculators from Tisfield, and owned by two or three small tradesmen in Arnington, are detestable styes, with their slate roofs, rubbishy doors and windows and scamped brickwork . . . unused front parlours. . . . The small kitchen at the back with an impracticable little range

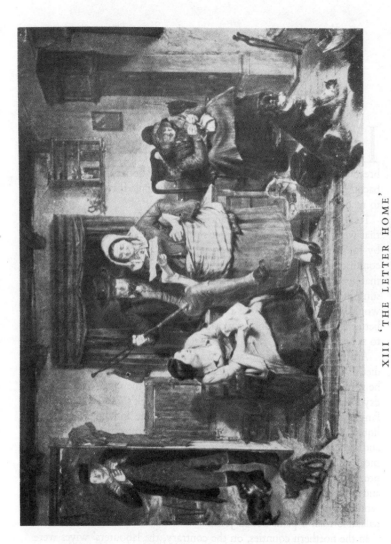

XIII 'THE LETTER HOME'

from a coloured engraving, c. 1860 (artist unknown) showing contemporary clothing and furniture. (Author's collection.)

XIV LODGE IN THE 'PICTURESQUE' STYLE (early 19th century)
from E. Bartell, *Hints for Picturesque Improvements in Ornamented Cottages*, 1804

... perhaps a copper as well, is often inhabited at one time by a family, of seven or eight souls, the dinner a-preparing and the week's wash half dried. Up the breakneck stairs there are two or three little bedrooms, stifling in summer, bitter in frost. The whole building, whether Jacobean or Victorian, reeks with a thick warm smell, compounded nastiness, preserved within well-closed windows. . . .'

Just before the First World War there were few cottages remaining with only one bedroom in Dorset, Essex, Kent, Somerset, Surrey, Wiltshire and Worcestershire, the majority, then old, having two, one of which was very small, and mostly there was no fire-place upstairs. New cottages in these counties invariably had three bedrooms, but few new ones were then being built, if we may accept J. L. Green on *English Country Cottages*. Privy accommodation was, however, still defective, there being only one to two or even three houses.

Aubrey Spencer reported that Kent cottages were usually in better repair than those in Dorset and Wiltshire in 1893, and that they had two down and two upstairs rooms, the new ones having three bedrooms. Here again there was an average of only one privy to two houses. Many old farmhouses in the county had 'of recent years' been converted into cottages and provided superior accommodation. Gardens were normal but there was no 'system of drainage' in most villages, and water supply was lamentably deficient on the hills, being dependent on roof catchment and tanks although there was not the same difficulty in the valleys.

Further west, in the Union of Basingstoke, the cottages were very varied in 1893, some having only one bedroom, and the reporter caustically remarks that some of the worst belonged to Oxford Colleges. The village of Ellisfield got its water supply from pools. Anna Lee Merritt describes Hurstbourne Tarrant near Andover, in *A Hamlet in Old Hampshire* (1902). 'The labourer's cottages . . . are little whitened huts, curiously compounded of bricks, timber, hurdles and mortar (called expressively wattle and daub) and covered with thatch. From a distance they are scarcely distinguishable from the ricks. Two or three tiny rooms shelter large families living by unceasing toil; toil which has no reward but daily bread, and hardly enough of that. And yet in this narrow home, affection and self-sacrifice find room enough.' At Beaulieu in the New Forest, the property of Lord Henry Scott, (afterwards Lord Montague of Beaulieu) every cottage had a living room, scullery and pantry and two or three bedrooms, with a good water supply and thorough drainage, pigsty and 20-pole of

I

garden at a rent of 1s. a week when Richard Heath (*The English Peasant*) visited the place about 1870.

It must have been the 'new' estate cottages (they had been going up for about a hundred years) that impressed writers like H. J. Little[1] and T. E. Kebbel. The former was convinced that a great improvement in cottages had taken place in the thirty years before 1878, although there were still some squalid, dirty and dilapidated, occasionally so bad as to be unfit for human habitation, but these were then 'most rare exceptions'. Little thought that the transfer of estates to parvenus the cause of good work in new cottages, and there may have been a spark of truth in the statement. Kingsley has something to say on the point. A new landlord annoyed everybody, not excluding the labourers for whom he provided new cottages, as part of his commercialization of an estate. Little says that on such estates the low mud and stud thatched tenement with its two rooms on the ground floor had almost entirely disappeared—whatever so qualified a phrase may mean. He provides plans and elevations of James Martin's prize cottages of 1869, the usual ideal, which had been in mind for more than twenty years.[2] The then 'present state of cottage accommodation was daily becoming a subject of greater satisfaction'.

Basing his argument partly on Little's report, partly on the Royal Commission on Agriculture, 1879–82, and partly on his own observation, Kebbel (*The Old and the New English Country Life*, 1891) says 'the labourer's cottages, as a rule, are far better than they used to be. . . . The hovels which still exist under the name of cottages almost always belong to the occupiers themselves, who sturdily refuse to quit them, or else to speculative builders in some adjoining town, who have run them up cheaply, and charge for them as dearly, as they can', which is a repetition of a very old contention.

Certainly there had been room for improvement, and the farther to the south-west the greater distance there was between the ideal and the real. In 1849 a good landlord was erecting earth closets in an attempt to bring the rudiments of sanitation to some Dorset cottages. Two farmers were riding by and one remarked on this state of luxury, 'I tell you what it is, James, they will be giving them horses to ride to work on next', or so Llewellyn Powys relates in his *Dorset Essays* (1935); and he tells how the Rev. Lord Sidney Osborne visited the

[1] H. J. Little, *The Agricultural Labourer* in *Journal of R. Agric. Soc.* (1878).

[2] C. W. Johnson and Edward Cressy, *The Cottages of Agricultural Labourers* (1847), p. 54.

wife of a Ryme Intrinsica labourer, who had stolen some corn, and found the woman with two of the children eating a few unwholesome potatoes and some bread; a child of 9 years of age, dead, in a coffin close to them; the only ascent to the bedroom by a broken ladder; the roof so dilapidated that it rains down on their bed.

Not all the great estates were good by 1893 when Aubrey J. Spencer reported that the Rivers estate and many other places were bad. There were a few cottages with one bedroom only. Where there were two they were small. One of these had bedrooms 6 ft. by 9 ft. and 10 ft. by 9 ft. and 6 ft. 2 in. high; the one downstairs room was 11 ft. by 9 ft. and 6 ft. 2 in. Another, slightly larger, had two bedrooms of 9 ft. by 10 ft. and one downstairs room 9 ft. by 15 ft. and 6 ft. 4 in. high. Some of the better cottages had three bedrooms. Many, says Spencer, had had nothing done to them since the 1867 Report, yet there had been some improvement in recent years since attention had been drawn to the cottage question. There was no general system of drainage except at Maiden Newton, but the earth closet had been 'pretty generally' adopted. Too often the wells were subject to pollution from surface water. Allotments were common, and potato ground was ploughed and manured free of charge. At Stourpaine, F. E. Green, *A History of the English Agricultural Labourer*, 1870–1920, citing Cobden, mentions a single bedroom where there were three beds, occupied by eleven people of all ages and both sexes, with no curtain or partition whatever, and at Milton Abbas, the eighteenth century model village, the over-crowding was even worse.

This sort of thing confirms the action of the Rev. Lord Sidney Osborne in Dorset, and of Canon Girdlestone, in arranging for the migration and emigration of the 'surplus' labourers to conditions in industrial towns which were probably little, if any better, or to frontier conditions in the colonies. The worst conditions in the West of England in 1872 are described in no honeyed words by Francis George Heath in *The English Peasantry* (1874).

Twenty years before that date another cleric, the Rev. W. H. Kerslake, had built cottages to the plans described by George Arnold, which won the prize of the Bath and West Society. This was near Crediton, and the cottages had a living room 13 ft. by 11 ft. 4 in., a scullery 14 ft. by 6 ft., a porch, a pantry and closet, three bedrooms 10 ft. by 11 ft., 7 ft. by 8 ft., and 10 ft. by 7 ft. with a fire-place in one of them. They cost £160 a pair. Four years after Heath's book Elias P. Squarey, writing on *Farm Capital* in the 'Royal' Journal of 1878, states that cottages usually had a living room and scullery or washing place with a small pantry on the ground floor, and three bedrooms over. If a large number is built, he remarks, about two in seven have only two bedrooms. He is probably thinking about cottages built on the great estates, because his opinion is that on smaller properties they were often inadequate. Squarey's county, Wiltshire, is very large and Spencer's 1893 Report on Pewsey Union is not so optimistic. The village itself was then in poor repair because it was the property of independent owners. On the Marquis of Ailesbury's estate there were some good new cottages with three bedrooms; some old ones had only one; but the majority had two. Ludgershall cottages were mostly old and dilapidated 'as in other places'. Two new ones, with two rooms downstairs 12 ft. by 14 ft. and 9 ft. by 12 ft. and 9 ft. high and three bedrooms 12 ft. square, 13 ft. by 12 ft. and 14 ft. by 8 ft. and 8 ft. high and provided with a washhouse, had cost £380. Most of the cottages in the Union had two bedrooms, very few one, and only a few more than these, three. Occasionally there was only one privy to two houses. Spencer found much the same conditions in the Langport Union, Somerset. At Honiton, an American Quaker, Elihu Burritt,[1] who made several lengthy 'pedestrian tours' in the 1860's, remarked clay floors in cottages where one room serves as parlour, kitchen, cellar and sometimes sleeping apartment. The Crediton Union, in which the Rev. Mr. Kerslake had been building model cottages so long before, was well supplied with cottages when Chapman reported in 1893. Most had two but a few had only one bedroom and new ones with three were gradually being built. Few bedrooms had fire-places, and a ceiling of 6 ft. 2 in. often sloped to 4 ft. with a window 'on the ground'. Earth closets were then being used in place of the old cesspools. There was no lack of water and good gardens. Some cottagers kept cows and many kept pigs. A year before, Hugh O'Neill published *Devonshire Idylls* and said that Kitty Comer's cottage at Little Comfort was just a kitchen back and front, with a lean-to on one side and a shippon on the other. Above, there were a couple of chambers and a sort of loft over the shippon. It was in a dilapidated state and rented at 1s. a week, but the labourer who took it put it in order in his spare time. On Dartmoor, so late as 1899 (S. Baring Gould, *A Book of the West*), there was an old moorman's granite cottage. The door opened into a storeroom cluttered up with potatoes, old barrels, cartwheels and poultry hopping to and fro over

---

[1] Elihu Burritt, *A Walk from London to Land's End and Back* (1865), p. 189.

all. On one side a door led to kitchen, hall and parlour all in one, lighted by a small window looking into the courtyard; on the other side was a cattle shed all under one roof and beyond the kitchen was the common sleeping chamber. There was no upper storey and in such a house it was rare to find one. An art school started by some philanthropist in one village was begun in a one-roomed cottage and gradually extended into the one-roomed cottage adjoining.

There were too few cottages in the Truro Union in 1893 and these were in a poor state of repair. Everywhere there were some with only one bedroom, although, as elsewhere, new ones had, usually three. The water supply was good, but privy accommodation was notable for its complete absence in many places. Few had gardens, and there was no demand for allotments.

How can all this evidence be summed up? It is only possible to say that by the end of the nineteenth century a great many cottages conforming to the modern ideal of five or six rooms had been built all over the country and these rooms were no smaller than those in many urban and suburban houses of more recent construction. There was often a regrettable absence of plumbing and a none too certain water supply. On the other hand it is probable that a majority of the cottages did not come within measurable distance of these standards. There were many of the one up and one down type, the upper room in some being reached by a ladder; but possibly the standard of the majority of rural dwellings was the four-roomed cottage. Similarly the physical conditions of the buildings varied greatly. Many were dilapidated and almost uninhabitable; repairs were at a discount, because, as E. N. Bennett puts it in *Problems of Village Life*, the rent it was possible for a labourer to pay yielded a percentage so small that cottage building passed out of the category of business into that of 'somewhat expensive philanthropy'.

X FURNITURE AND CLOTHING

LITTLE enough can be discovered about the quantities and types of furniture and clothing owned by the labourers and their families during the Victorian era; perhaps that is because these quantities were little enough. A great deal has been written, for example, about the utility of the smock frock and doubtless it was a serviceable garment, particularly when it was made of thick layers of material that made it waterproof. A trifle unfortunately it has come to be regarded as a romantic covering, and none of the contemporary or modern writers who sing its praises took the trouble to state whether each person owned one or six smocks or how often it was necessary to replace a worn-out garment with a new one. It is, however, exceedingly likely that any labourer above the poverty line, and there must have been a few, owned two, one for working days and one for Sundays. Other garments were probably owned in much the same quantities, but one thing is certain, no more were owned than in the eighteenth century, for which time it was possible to find a few detailed estimates. A general statement was made by H. J. Little in the 'Royal' Journal essay of 1878, already referred to. The labourer then wore trousers and coat of corduroy or fustian, or breeches and gaiters of stout leather, a loose cotton neckerchief round his neck and stout heavily nailed boots. He must also have had some kind of a hat, but these details omit the relevant particulars of state of repair, period of replacement and so on, and they say nothing of the situation of the wife and children. The man's Sunday clothes were of broadcloth with a gorgeous waistcoat of crimson plush, ornamented with countless buttons. It is worth while noting that Little lived at Wisbech.

That the corduroy and fustian of everyday were supplemented by a Sunday suit about seventy or eighty years ago is confirmed by a memory recorded by C. Henry Warren in *The Happy Countryman* (1939). A labourer told him that his wife's father then used to grace the

village on Sundays in a pair of white moleskin cloth breeches below
which he wore a pair of white leggings fastened up the sides with
mother of pearl buttons. His boots were elastic sided—'a fashion
common with the men, at least on high days and holidays, as well as
with the women. "And very pretty he looked too." ' Again Alfred
Williams writing *Round About the Upper Thames* (1922) mentions one
Shadrack, a labourer, who wore a white corduroy suit at approxi-
mately the same date. And 'Leather Breeches' was the nickname of an
old man in that district. The buckskin breeches that he wore, 'according to a carefully preserved tradition, had been in the family for a
hundred years, and as well as being wrinkled and withered with age
... were filthy with grease. People said that all he had to eat with his
barley bread was fat from his breeches got by frizzling them before
the fire.' The widespread use of this garment is shown by the Rev.
J. C. Atkinson's remark that the hereditary leather breeches of the
labourer had quite gone out of fashion by 1891 in the village of Danby,
Cleveland.[1] And breeches were not the only article that became
heirlooms. George Baldry, the author of *The Rabbit Skin Cap* (1939),
tells a story of an old East Anglian labourer he knew in his childhood
about the 1860's or 1870's who was never seen without a long-sleeved
waistcoat inherited from his father or grandfather, who always made
his wife patch it up when it got worn or torn, and who insisted finally
on being buried in it.

These memories are confirmed by William Coles Finch, *Life in
Rural England*, and he also gives an idea of how long an outfit was
expected to last. 'These dear old people,' he says of the labouring class
of the decade 1880–90, 'wore with pride and spoke with pride of
certain clothes which they purchased when they were married, and
were proud in the knowledge that they would serve for many years.
In those days fashion did not change with the moon, and if it had
changed they would have ignored it.' Later on he supplies the same
details of the man's dress as others, i.e. corduroy breeches, gaiters or
worsted stockings and heavy boots, a handkerchief round the neck
and a soft felt hat. On Sundays the best smock frock and a tall hat
were usual, or, if he had a wedding suit that would become his Sunday
suit for life. A bailiff was dressed no differently.

All these things were excellent so long as they were in good repair,
but the best material will wear out in time, and garments have a way of

[1] Rev. J. C. Atkinson, *Forty Years in a Moorland Parish* (1891), p. 5.

wanting replacement all together, to the confusion of the domestic economy based on a small budget. By the 80's, it is possible, though not altogether likely, that the labourer's clothing was always replaced at sufficient intervals, but twenty years before then this was not so. Alexander Somerville a former ploughman, visited many different districts and recorded what he saw in *The Whistler at the Plough* (1852). At Heyshot, West Sussex, Cobden's birthplace, he gave pennies to the children in a cottage he entered because he was speaking to a child whose toes were out of its shoes, whose pinafore was torn, or whose clothing was otherwise scanty and much worn, 'and unhappily we may go over many miles of country and across some entire counties, and not alight on a family where this is not the condition of the children's clothes'. There was, of course, always a difficulty in finding the money to buy new clothes out of the minute wages earned by the farm labourer at this date, and indeed much later, and had it not been for the charity of the upper classes, the difficulty might have proved insurmountable. H. G. O'Neill, whose *Devonshire Idylls* (1892) I have mentioned, remarks: 'Our worn garments made Sunday coats and frocks for the little ones . . . and ready made baby clothes were always a welcome gift to a busy mother.'

In the neighbouring county of Dorset the men wore tidy coats of black or blue and tall beavers on Sunday when Richard Heath was there in 1872, while the women were simply but neatly attired, a sign, he thought, of the gentle breeding of the Dorset peasant. William Barnes writes of such an one—

> Last Easter Jim put on his blue
> Frock cwoat the vu'st time—vier new;
> Wi' yollow buttons all o' brass,
> That glittered in the zun lik' glass.
> And pok'd 'ithin the button hole
> A tutty he'd a'begg'd or stole.
> A span new wes'co't, too, he wore,
> Wi' yollow stripes all down avore,
> An' tied his breeches' lags below
> The knee, wi' ribbon in a bow;
> An' drow'd his kitty-boots azide,
> An' put his laggens on, an' tied
> His shoes wi' strings two vinkers wide,
>   Because 'twer Easter Zunday.

His girl for whom he arrayed himself in all this splendour—

> Her frocks be a-meade all becomen an' plain
> An' clean as a blossom undimmed by a stain.
> Her bonnet ha' got but two ribbons, a-tied
> Up under her chin, or let down at the zide.

The Cornish labourer had only one outfit for everyday wear, consisting of a coarse shirt, a pair of duck trousers not quite reaching to the ankles, a duck smock and low quartered shoes, according to A. K. Hamilton Jenkin.

By what means did the labourers accumulate money out of their scanty earnings to buy clothing with? The Report of 1893 answers this question in part. It contains a fairly large number of detailed estimates of labourers' weekly income and expenditure. When there were grown-up sons the problem was more readily solved. Two Northumberland families faired well. One consisted of a father, mother, an adult son and another of seventeen, besides three younger children. Their clothes cost them all a total of £24 2s. 9½d. in 1891, made up of drapery goods £3 9s. 9d., boots £2 15s. 3d. and clothes (unspecified) £17 17s. 9½d. The other, of practically identical make-up, spent £25 3s. 4d. from May, 1889, to May, 1890, made up of tailor's bill £13; boots £5 10s.; sundry small articles £1 13s. 4d.; underclothing £5.

An Isle of Ely labourer bought every second year a working jacket at £1 6s.; breeches and gaiters at £1; sleeved waistcoat at 14s.; and every year two shirts at 8s.; one jersey at 5s. 3d.; one pair of stockings; a cap at 1s. 6d.; boots at 14s. 3d. Another, a single man, bought Sunday clothing every fourth year costing £3 2s. 6d. Some of these estimates are certainly impossible, particularly one dealing with the family of a man in the same county, who was ill all the year, his wife and four children at home, out of a total of seven. These are said to have spent on dress annually; the man £1; the woman £2 10s.; Daniel, a son, £4; Sarah, a daughter, £3 10s.; three younger children £4 10s. They also bought each year one pair of sheets at 8s.; teacloths at 8d. each; two towels at 7d.; two pillowcases at 2s. The weekly spending of this family is put at £1 6s. 2d., but even with charitable assistance this is an unlikely figure, especially when the father was unable to earn.

Many of the more careful labourers paid small sums into a clothing club weekly to provide a sum from which necessities could be bought. The subscription ranged from 6d. up to 2s. or even 3s. according to the family's earning capacity. The total annual spending was up to £4 with another £2 or so on boots. Some saved at home but often enough the weekly sum could not be put in the old teapot because daily appetites had proved too hearty. When saving in any form proved impossible what boots and clothes that were bought had to come out of extra earnings at piece work, or out of the harvest money, if that was not already earmarked for rent. Even so, a Nottinghamshire labourer's wife had to make a pair of boots last two years, her husband having a new pair every year. Charity was a usual supplement, or customary gifts by the farmer formed what, in fact, was a part of wages. This was so in Hereford, where a family of man, wife and six children, including one boy earning 6s. a week, spent £2 19s. on boots annually; £3 10s. on clothes and in addition received every other Christmas help with the children's shoes, a coat and trousers for father and a blanket and flannel for the house. A similar family was given the same gifts and a cast-off dress for making gowns for the children. It spent £2 12s. on boots and £3 on clothing. Details of the annual cost of clothes for another Hereford family of man, wife and six children are: Boots—nine pairs for £2 0s. 6d.; jacket, waistcoat, trousers, hat, two shirts, scarf and three pairs of stockings for £1 10s. 4d.; two pairs of sheets for 7s.; 24 yards of calico for 7s.; fourteen pairs of stockings 6s. 5d.; 21 yards of flannel for 14s.; 18 yards of dress stuff for 9s.; six hats at 5½d. each, 2s. 9d.; 8 yards of dress stuff for wife at 4s.; two pairs of stockings for 1s. The inclusion of a new hat for the man every year is a suspicious item in this statement, and it may have been compiled by a farmer, as so many of them were. The fact probably is, as F. E. Green puts it, new clothes were an event, and they lasted many years, and, indeed the scale of the labourer's earnings forbade any great continuous spending on dress, except that boots must be had.

Everyone is agreed that the young single man was better off than the married man when both were earning the same weekly wage, and that is a palpable truism; so the single man was able to save money towards setting up a home. Few were so poor as the young couple mentioned by E. C. Hayden, in *Travels Round Our Village (Berkshire)* (1905), who set up house 'with the modest outfit of a bed and a saucepan'. This seems to have been in Hampshire. At Sheepscombe, in Gloucestershire, a village described by Mary Roberts, a lesser known Miss Mitford, in 1831 (*Annals of My Village*) the inside of a whitewashed cottage displayed a neat set of china, the housewife's pride, in a corner cupboard; a high-back leather chair for the 'gude-man'; and the 'auld family bible' on a bright rubbed oaken stand; the furniture, though coarse, was clean, and various little ornaments upon the walls. This was a prosperous family, because there was a pig in the sty and a well-filled rabbit box in the shed, and the scene is very different from that described by Cobbett in Leicestershire.

Forty years later Richard Heath was in Northumberland, and noted the furniture in a one-roomed cot. In one corner there was a large bedstead, a family heirloom, completely shrouded by white dimity; there was a box bed for the children. The mahogany furniture bright with polish, he adds, the display of crockery and ornaments, the easy comfort of every arrangement—attest the fact they are not poor. In another there was a spotless deal table, a large oven in a range put in by the tenant, a looking-glass and a case of shelves for the carefully arranged crockery and two box beds. A Yorkshire cottage possessed a tall mahogany clock in the spotlessly clean parlour, a shorter clock and barometer. The burnished steel of the range was dazzling and the room was adorned with numerous mourning cards framed and glazed, and two rocking chairs.

Heath, of course, covered a good deal of country. At Shottery, Ann Hathaway's village, an old couple were living alone in a two-roomed cottage. They had a tall clock in a very clean room, a rack with some willow pattern plates, and some small religious pictures. Presumably they also had chairs, a table and a bed, but these items are not mentioned. At Wootten, Oxford, the great four-poster bed touched the ceiling. It was most likely a discarded piece from a richer house which had found its 'last refuge with the rural poor'. There were many gaudy little pictures and a quantity of crockery. Heath remarks the flower pots on window sills, but enumerates no more details.

The kitchen of R. D. Blackmore's *Cripps the Carrier*, who lived in Buckinghamshire about the same time, was a good sized room and 'very picturesque with snugness'. There was a dresser with brass-handled drawers that seemed quietly nursing table cloths, a warming pan, a grand chair, the arm-chair of yew-tree and a clock. Next door, but a rather distant next door, in the Vale of the White Horse, Thomas Hughes describes, in *Tom Brown's Schooldays*, a farmer's cottage which was very like those of the better class of peasantry in general. A snug chimney corner with two seats, and a small carpet on the hearth, an old flint gun and a pair of spurs over the fire-place, a dresser with shelves on which some bright pewter plates and crockery ware were arranged, an old walnut table, a few chairs and settles (? how many), some framed samplers and an old print or two, and a bookcase with some dozen volumes on the walls, a rack with flitches of bacon and other stores fastened to the ceiling, and 'you have the best part of the furniture'.

Quite a different atmosphere is created by John Halsham's description of Old Tomsett's kitchen at *Idlehurst*, Sussex, in 1897. The kitchen was of the common pattern, a low ceiling of dusty plaster and black timbers, rickety windows with leaded panes, one battered door to the outer air. The sempiternal kettle bubbled on the stove; a cat dozed on the faded patchwork cushion in the armchair; a couple of photographs and a stuffed plover graced the walls. Over all hung the dull fustiness mixed of damp foundations, rotting thatch, wood fires, cooking and old corduroy. The lattice, patched with brown paper, looked on a garden plot of withered kale-stumps and a moss-covered apple tree. By the fire, sitting upright, stick in hand, in round frock, long gaiters and an ancient billy-cock hat, was Tomsett who, by the way, was 80 years old. Halsham was doubtful whether any comprehensive tubbing was possible in such a kitchen, and indeed it is unlikely after babyhood. Richard Heath comments that the people of Sussex were very clean as a rule. The men wore black smocks and the women were neat in their dress. The cottage interiors were black with wood smoke just as they were 300 years before, but the floors and seats were scrupulously clean. A chain hung kettle was in the open chimney and a settle in front. At Rotherfield, in a two-bedroom cottage, he saw a miserable bed almost on the floor and in the small outer room a shake-down for the children. 'Not a chair—nor a table was in the room.' It is no wonder that of ten children the woman bore she had only been able to 'raise' two.

A Dorset cob cottage, 20 ft. wide, had the floor sanded and was furnished with tall chairs and an ancient escritoire from Corfe, a couple of fire dogs and a Bible. There was a stack of 3,000 peats for firing which had cost 3s. a thousand.

Luckett's Place, Wiltshire, is described by Richard Jefferies in *Round About a Great Estate* (1880). 'The kitchen had perhaps originally been the house, the rest having been added to it in the course of years. . . . The walls were quite 4 ft. thick and the one small lattice window in its deep recess scarcely let in sufficient light, even on a summer's day, to dispel the gloom except at one particular time. The little panes, yellow and green, were but just above the ground. . . . There was an old oak table in the centre of the room—a table so solid that young

Aaron, the strong labourer, could lift it only with difficulty. . . .'
Alfred Williams adds something for Wiltshire. The home of Mark
Titcombe, in *A Wiltshire Village* (1912), was simplicity itself. There
was one very large room downstairs, kitchen, parlour and living
room combined. The floor of large and small flat stones was whitened
with free stone. The open hearth had a bread oven halfway up the
chimney on one side. A cupboard adjoined the fire-place on the other.
There were three small deal tables and three straight-backed chairs,
and painted clay figures of animals on the mantelpiece. A few pieces
of old china on shelves had belonged to his mother. The old clock
was silent. There were two bedrooms above, but the furniture there
is not catalogued. Williams' *Round About the Upper Thames* (1922)
says that a fair type of the average home of a Cotswold labourer was
a cottage of four rooms. Such was a carter's cottage where only one
of the downstairs rooms was the general living room, the other only
being used in summer. The living room was furnished with a large
deal table, an ancient sofa covered with faded red cloth, a chest of
drawers and half a dozen chairs, including the armchair by the fire.
There was an old-fashioned oak folding table just inside the door, and
a great many pictures (nearly 100 photos) and ornaments, some fifty
on the mantel. The carter's family of twelve had all left home.

Walter White, who made *A Londoner's Walk to the Land's End*, in
1855, slept in a shoemaker's cottage at Nachers, near Newton Ferrars,
Devon. The bedroom he slept in was low and open to the thatch but
was clean; the mahogany four-post bed had clean sheets; there was
a washstand properly furnished and towels without stint. The shoemaker was a little better off than the average farm labourer. He sold
ginger beer with his trade, put up an occasional traveller, and with his
pig and his garden was pretty comfortable.

A. K. Hamilton Jenkin has appropriated Cornwall as his subject and
provides varying descriptions of conditions in that county in his
Cornish Homes and Customs (1934). Quoting Bottrell's *Folk Tales* he
relates a story of how a family managed to sleep 150 years ago. 'The
babies,' said the woman, 'I do put in the costan (straw basket), the
small ones get up on the talfat (a plank ledge built half-way up the
wall) and stretch themselves in the bed, round the bed and under the
bed, as they like,' and there was a bunk in the corner. In the more
prosperous cottages the pewter that was formerly to be seen on the
kitchen dresser had usually vanished by 1850. On the farms the kitchen
was furnished with a long table and benches quite in the ancient style, the

children being accommodated in a low window seat. There was usually a large settle for three or four persons, a grandfather or Dutch clock, a warming pan, flour hutch, pitchers, bellows, salt box and candle box and herbs hanging from the rafters. The back kitchen was usually a lean-to: the less prosperous had a rude table in the one downstairs room, with possibly three or four straight-backed chairs; the majority, however, used the long form and a three-legged stool while the children sat on blocks of wood. There were a few earthenware cups, saucers and basins, some wooden or tin plates, an iron crock for boiling and a kettle or baker. The bedroom furniture was equally scanty, only a couple of bedsteads with crossed ropes to support the matress.

Naturally enough there was never any surplus of clothes or furniture in the possession of the farm labourer of the Victorian era. His wages did not permit of any extravagance in either direction, and very many labouring families must have been helped towards the minimum necessities of clothing by charitable gifts of other's cast-offs, particularly the women and children. As for the furniture, what was not inherited was most certainly second- or more hand, and though none the worse for that, was probably in no very reputable state of repair until it had been patched up by the head of the family, or it was the cumbersome pieces which newer fashions had ousted in turn from the great house and the farm house.

XI FOOD

I HAVE already made it clear that individual memory, unsupported, by accurate and detailed notes made at the time memory is recalling, is no very trustworthy indication of the less remote past. Many persons of many times have recalled to memory the times of their childhood perhaps fifty years before they were writing. Living memory can do little more than that, and is confined to the '90's or at most the '80's of last century, but there are early records of memories of childhood and they can be stretched over most of the Victorian era. What are they, and how do they compare with contemporary records?

The well-known broadcaster, the late C. H. Middleton, issued his *Village Memories* in 1941, and recalled a time fifty years before when the village was worth living in. He does not believe the standard of living among the labourers was lower than it is to-day. 'Don't you believe it.' The food eaten was more wholesome and palatable. All meat was home killed, so he says, and each family had one weekly joint, making up with pig-meat, a rabbit or poultry, and nearly every labourer kept a pig. Fortunately the Royal Commission on Labour (1893) printed a large number of weekly budgets of farm labourers, and these can be used to check the accuracy of this halcyon statement of affairs.

In 1909 Peter Durrant, an old labourer, 'simply a voice with a memory,' told Edward Thomas (*The Heart of England*) that he doted on roast pork though it was not often to be had. Once when he was about fifty, a time that must be not too far from Middleton's 'fifty years ago', 'he had been threshing all morning and had eaten no food, and there was none in the house . . . stopped work and took a walk round the farmyard. There he saw a fat pig lying on its side . . . lifting up his flail he began to thresh the pig, and shouting above its screams: Son of a fool, I'll teach you to eat my dinner. Nor did he cease . . . until the farmer came out and pitying his case, sent him out a dish of roast pork to make amends.' Another old labourer said of the period of the Crimea War, 'bad times they were. But we had tea, we had tea; the wife used to grate up toast and pour boiling water on it'. 'We called that coffee,' said the youngest, a lover of truth.

An old Hampshire woman recounted happier memories of a slightly earlier day to W. H. Hudson in 1902 (*Hampshire Days*). 'I've made elderberry wine years and years and years,' she said. 'So did my mother; so did my grandmother; so did everybody in my time. . . . But no-body wants it now. . . . Nothing's good enough now unless you buys it in a public house or a shop. It wasn't so when I was a girl. We did everything for ourselves and it were better, I tell 'e. We kep' a pig then—so did everyone; and the pork and brawn it were good, not like what we buy now. We put it mostly in brine, and let it be for months; and when we took it out and boiled it, it were red as a cherry and white as milk, and it melted just like butter in your mouth. That's what we ate in my time. But you can't keep a pig now. . . . We've got very partickler about smells now. . . .

'And we didn't drink no tea then (8s. a lb.). . . . We had beer for breakfast then and it did us good. It were better than all these nasty cocoa stuffs we drinks now. . . . And we had a brick oven then and could put a pie in and a loaf and whatever we wanted and it were proper vittals. We baked barley bread and black bread and all sorts of bread and it did us good and made us strong. These iron ranges and stoves we have now—what's the good o' they? You can't bake bread in 'em. And the wheat bread you gits from the shop, what's it good for? 'Tisn't proper vittals—it fills 'em with wind.'

Just before the First World War Christopher Holdenby got first-hand experience of the lot of the farm labourers by working as one, and recorded this part of his life in *Folk of the Farm*. He lodged with a farm worker and ate with the family. The tea was strong 'with that rough-ness which sets one's teeth on edge. It was only made palatable with at least four lumps of sugar, or rather two dessert-spoonfuls. And the bread and butter, of course it was always cut, and I often wondered that "the mother" even found time to do anything else but dispense our staple diet. Yet she did, and I have even known her produce home-made gingerbread and pastry. I learned well the method of combining cheese and pickles, and I became an excellent judge of the flavour of potatoes. The great thing, if possible, is to find gravy from somewhere in which to crush the potatoes, and for this purpose my friends usually produced something they called "meat". There was not much of it,

XV OLD AND NEW FARM COTTAGES, 1848
from W. J. Gray, *Treatise on Rural Architecture*, 1852

XVI FARM WORKERS IN THE FIELD
showing contemporary clothing.
From L. G. Seguin, *Rural England*, 1885

XVII DESIGNS FOR 'GOOD NOT CHEAP' COTTAGES

from John Vincent, *Country Cottages*, 1861

and I doubt if there would have been any without a lodger, and it was so cooked as to extract all the goodness, I would defy anyone but a butcher to name whence these dainties came and from what beast, though I increased my knowledge considerably about the muscles and sinews of our vertebrates. Once a week we often had "a decent piece of meat" and the family knew how to appreciate it. There are thousands of cottages where they do not always see fresh meat once a week. I have lived in one such. . . . The other staple article of food was bacon. . . . We did not even waste the rind. . . . Our great treat was tinned herrings on Saturday nights'. Of course if there was a garden with some fruit trees, the vegetables and fruit could be added to this regimen. This is not memory but experience, and there is a good deal more recorded experience throughout the century.

When Cobbett visited his grandmother he got only bread and milk for breakfast, apple pudding for dinner and bread and cheese for supper[1], and the Reports of Select Committees, etc., of his day show that in many districts bread was often the chief food during the decade 1821–31, some families being unable to supply themselves even with cheese or potatoes. Tea was only drunk 'when they could get it', and in 1850 Caird[2] observed that where wages were lowest bread, potatoes, cheese occasionally, and hot water poured over burnt crusts, was the staple food, while the 1867 Report states that the most underfed counties were Dorset, Kent, Chester, Salop, Stafford and Rutland. Bacon was the luxury of the comparatively well-to-do. Francis Heath found the same conditions in North Devon in 1874.

There were marked differences as between families and these are, of course, reflected in the evidence. At Danby, Cleveland, the people depended mainly on the farm produce for sustenance, when the Rev. J. C. Atkinson went there about 1850. The butchers killed once a week, sold the little that was called for locally and the rest in Whitby Market on Saturday. The bacon, bread, potatoes and milk produced on the farms supplied much the larger part of the diet of master and servant alike, and conditions were much the same in 1890.

In a North Country Village M. E. Francis waxes eloquent about the gratifying odour of cooking bacon at Thornleigh, in 1896: 'bacon is the staff of life—for breakfast in the morning, a slab or two cold and sometimes raw, between two thick slices of bread for "baggin" or lunch, and again, as often as not, for dinner (when the last of the Sunday

[1] Esther Meynell, Country Ways (1942).
[2] James Caird, English Agriculture in 1850–1 (1852).

K

beef has been disposed of) cooked before the fire, in a deep dish, and served up smoking and savoury with "taters" in the gravy.' The 'gradeley' farmer had Irish stew or 'toad in the hole', but bacon is the staple food of the cottagers, and they certainly seem to thrive on it.

Bacon was not, however, so usual in Suffolk fifty years before. *Margaret Catchpole,* a young female peasant, the fiction of Richard Cobbold, was one of those who 'bound to meet a parent or a brother at the welcome hour of noon, bearing the frugal dinner of bread and cheese or it may sometimes chance to be, bread and pork'. The funeral baked meats prepared by a sorrowing widow of the same class here consisted of some cake, bread and butter, a cup of tea and a pint of beer each for the men.

George Baldry, who spent his boyhood in the adjoining county of Norfolk, recalls that his breakfast as a boy (he was 66 in 1939 when his *Rabbit Skin Cap* appeared) was salt sop. This was a few pieces of bread crumbled into a basin with small pieces of butter, lard or dripping and hot water poured over it—a dish referred to as 'tea kettle broth' in my ·childhood in Dorset. Baldry's childhood memories were mostly of food as 'often there wasn't any'. A great feast was swedes boiled with Norfolk dumplings—he was given the swede by a shepherd whose flock he had helped to feed. Supper was a crust and skim milk. One Sunday dinner was a sheep's head, won by his shoemaker father in a raffle, and made into a stew with dumplings. He had also drunk burnt crust tea; the real article was only for the rich. Home brewed beer and home baked bread were other articles of diet.

An unfortunate woman at Heyshot told Alexander Somerville[1] that the harvest money had gone to pay the rent of the cottage in 1852, and they had been forced to sell their pig to pay for the husband's shoes, although they really should have eaten it themselves. Nearby at Dunford, another woman told him that they would die in the winter were it not for the potatoes grown in the garden: they only ate bread in addition.

A Kentish supper table, noticed by Richard Heath twenty years later, supported a more substantial meal of beefsteak pudding, bread and milk and all drank several cups of tea, but at Mayfield the eight children's dinner was only a dole of bread and cheese. Such poverty did not vanquish charity if an old Sussex song is not mere poetry.

[1] Alexander Somerville, *The Whistler at the Plough* (1852), pp. 402–4.

My board is simply spread,
I have a little food to spare,
But thou shalt break my wholesome bread,
And have a wholesome share.
For while the faggot burns
To warm my cottage floor,
They never shall say the poor man turns
A poorer from his door.

Perhaps it was about this time that an old labourer told John Halsham of the advantages gained by the poorly paid labourers if the cottage was favourably placed. 'Half the people in Arnton village thinks,' he said, 'as how they've only just learnt what's good to eat and that we old 'uns used to live on tater peelings. When I was a boy we used to live in a bit of a wood where there was a brook running by, and a lot of wet meadows and sallys growing about. My father he was won'erful clever with traps and he'd a gun—the keepers didn't say much generally —and most days we'd a hare (we didn't make much account of rabbits they was so common) or a pheasant he'd pick up a day or two after a shoot, and we'd wild duck sometimes; and I got trout out of the brook sometimes up to a pound and a half and eels; and we'd plenty of honey, and allus eggs; and apples most years round to Easter; and then the nuts and the mushrooms. They's plenty of people nowadays (1897) as don't live better than that.' His comment was very true, but the family must have been exceptionally well placed for taking *feræ* without punishment and they could not possibly have fared so well all the year round—another wealthy memory.

Mark Thurston, another old labourer, speaking of his boyhood about 1870, told C. Henry Warren of other conditions. Free blood and a pennyworth of suet from the butcher made blackpuddings for the family. Meat as a rule meant what we now call offal, the heart, liver and lungs of a beast, and cost about 10*d*. It was made up into various dishes and made to eke out a week. Lamb's tail puddings was another well-liked dish, but these were 'tasty feasts in a year long Lent of bread and potatoes'. If Mrs. Thurston was able to boil up some dumplings and a scrap of pork for her husband's tea, Mark got a couple of 'floaters' for his supper. 'A pinch of flour dipped in the water in which the dumplings were boiling, was rolled out between the thumb and the ball of the hand to about the size of a biscuit, fried and then sprinkled with a spoonful of sugar.' Bloaters could occasionally be got at two for 1½*d*.

A Blandford, Dorset, shepherd's wife, the mother of twelve children, seven of whom were living at home, told Richard Heath that they lived on potatoes, bread and pigmeat; often on dry bread, and that they had no milk. They drank cocoa at harvest. Near Dorchester the cottagers lived mainly on bread, cheese and potatoes, but they killed a pig occasionally. One of William Barnes' poems amply confirms this. The wife tells the labourer husband:

> Your supper's nearly ready. I've agot
> Some teaties here a-doen in the pot;
> I wish wi' all my heart I had some meat.
> I've got a little ceake, too, here a-beaken on
> Upon the vier. 'Tis done by this time, though;
> He's nice and moist; vor when I were a meakin o'n,
> I stuck some bits of apple in the dough.

For some reason several people have discussed Wiltshire farm labourers' regimen. An old couple living between Alton Barnes and Lockeridge remembered conditions in their childhood when A. G. Bradley was preparing his *Round About Wiltshire* (1907). They were then between 77 and 78 years old, so that their story relates to the times about 1840. They touched no meat, nor wheaten bread and no tea or sugar, or scarcely any. 'A little bacon was managed each week; but that was reserved for the man of the family, as engaged in the more strenuous labours; the women and children never touched it. Speaking of her father's household and her girlhood, the old woman told me they only had wheaten bread for a treat, barley bread and a sort of thin tea made from barley meal was the staple diet,' just as Richard Heath, about 1870, found that Northumbrian labourers' bread was made of barley and pea-meal, as it was some 200 years before. Another Wiltshire labourer, who had been transported to Bermuda for poaching, told Alexander Somerville in 1852 that he had terrible good living there: fresh beef three times a week, pork and peas four times. He wished he could have had such an allowance at home, but it was impossible on 8s. a week. Workhouse diet in this country, low as it is, comments Somerville, is better than half the Wiltshire workers got at home, and this is confirmed by Elihu Burritt's conversation with a man living between Swindon and Marlborough in 1864. He had worked on the same estate for thirty years at a regular wage of 8s. a week with an extra shilling at haymaking, 'and in all that time had never had a piece of fresh beef or mutton cooked under his roof. His

family being small he had a bit of bacon two or three times a week,'
and was proud to say that he had never had any parish relief. Another
memory, which may be personal but is not distinctly said to be, is
Atwood Clark's, of a Wiltshire carter in the '70's, recorded in *Country
Mixture* (1934). For breakfast this man had a drink of clear well water
and a half-warmed mess of porridge with a small slice of bread crumbled
into it. At midday dinner there was no cloth on the table, which was
scrubbed white. About an average meal in quantity and quality was
a pot three parts full of liquor and two large swedes, with 5 lb. or 6 lb.
of potatoes in their skins and a rind of bacon for flavouring. 'No bread
for you to-day,' the wife told her husband; 'children had to have it
this morning.' She couldn't manage another loaf that week; boots for
Mary, a daughter, were wanted, and 6d. a week must be saved whenever possible towards this necessity. This man, when working late got
an occasional meal at the farm, and a present of cake and skim milk
to take home. Richard Jefferies adds a footnote. 'Even in recent years,
now and then a servant upon entering service at the farmhouse, would
refuse to touch butcher's meat. She had never tasted anything but
bacon at home, and could only be persuaded to eat fresh meat with
difficulty, being afraid she would not like it. . . . They sometimes had
lettuce pudding for dinner and thought nothing of eating raw bacon.'
The meal for 'barley dodkins', 'barley scowters' and 'barley bangers',
or pot cakes, was usually shaken through a piece of coarse muslin, but
two old ladies, Sarah George and Moll Higgins improved on this
method. They sifted the meal through their Sunday bonnets. 'Bang
belly,' Williams says, was milk well stiffened with wheaten flour, and
frog water was the old familiar burnt crust tea. Old Mark Titcombe,
another of Williams' friends already referred to, ate only two meals
a day in 1912, breakfast and dinner combined at noon and tea about six.
His food was bread and a little butter, lard, cheese, or boiled bacon and
potatoes.

Passing into Somerset, Alexander Somerville noted that the wages
of the labourer in full employment were 7s. 6d. a week in 1852. '. . . for
years past their daily diet is potatoes for breakfast, dinner and supper,
and potatoes only. This year they are not living on potatoes because
they have none (the crop failed), and the wretched farm labourers
are now existing on half diet, made on barley meal, turnips, cabbages,
and such small allowance of bread as small wages will procure.' Bradley,
in his *Exmoor Memories* (1926) says that wages were up to 11s. a week
in the last year of the American Civil War, and goes on: 'They (the

labourers) just managed to exist and merely fell out of work or were on the parish in bad times. That was all. . . .'

H. C. O'Neill's Kitty Corner, of Little Comfort, Devon, fed on taties and green stuff from the garden. Keeping a pig was none so great an addition to the family food. The pig made 8 score and they sold the loin for 6s. They lived on chitterlings for pretty nigh a month, sold hog's puddings to the vicarage and pickled the rest. They never ate meat, but filled up on dumplings when the pork was done. They kept bees, but sold the honey except what was kept to make metheglin. They used sticks and furze stumps for firing.

All these recorded memories and experiences give some general idea of the dietary conditions under which the cottager lived during the Victorian era. More detailed and precise information is provided by estimated budgets from 1863 onwards, but unfortunately the investigators who published these budgets were content to collect them from people who were not themselves cottagers. For instance, the *Report of the Medical Officer of the Privy Council on the Food of the Poorer Labouring Classes* in 1863 contains a large number of these: they were, however, furnished by landowners, farmers, Local Government Board inspectors, members of Local Authorities, the clergy, relieving officers, tradesmen and agricultural labourers. They may, therefore, be biased in one way or another, either making the conditions look better than they were or worse, although there is always the possibility that they were accurate.

The average family in 1863 bought the following quantities weekly. The weights are given in decimal fractions because that is the easiest way to calculate an average. They relate to 370 unidentified families of an unstated composition:

	1863.	H. J. Little in 1878.
	lb.	lb.
Bacon	4·55	4·0
Bread	55·75	35·0 including flour
Potatoes	27	none
Cheese	1.5	none
Butter	1·56	·5 + 1 lb. lard
Tea, coffee or cocoa ..	0·14	·25
Sugar	2	2·5
Milk (pints)	1·75	none

Little's, a similar estimate of the expenditure of an individual 'hard-up'

family, is given in 1878, above for ready comparison. This family is
supposed to consist of a man, wife and four children, the eldest being
16. His characteristic comment is that it takes the whole income of the
man (13s. 9¾d. out of 14s. a week) to maintain him. 'The thriftless
character of English cottage house-keeping will be deducted from this
table. The English labourer's wife has seldome an idea of the preparation
of those savory pottages and messes which form so prominent a feature
in the cookery of Continental households.' Little was a large-scale
farmer near Wisbech.

Canon Tuckwell made a similar estimate for the same size family in
1885, which he says included bare necessities only. It is, weekly:

	£	s.	d.
Rent, including garden and pigsty		2	0
Bread, 8 loaves, 4d.–4½d.		2	10
Flour			9
Meat, 6 lb. at 8d. (bacon probably)		4	0
Potatoes			10
Cheese, 1 lb. at 8d.			8
Sugar, 2 lb. at 3d.			6
Tea, ½ lb. at 2s.		1	0
Butter, 1 lb. at 1s.		1	0
Milk		1	0
Treacle			3
Salt and pepper			2
Candles and paraffin			6
Fuel		1	6
Clothes, washing material, repairs, etc. ..		2	8
Tools, furniture, sundries			10
	£1	0	6

'Dreary England,' he remarks, 'had taken the place of Merrie
England,' but when the change, if there was such a change, took place
is not altogether determined. These budgets, however, do not precisely
confirm Kebbell's description of conditions at this time. 'The average
day-labourer,' he says, 'in regular work now eats butcher's meat
much oftener than he used to do. He will often have broiled ham for
breakfast; and at harvest time, when his wife, or oftener his little girl,
carries out "father's tea" to him in the meadows, if you lift the corner

of her apron (something of an impertinence), or peep into her basket, ten to one you will find a tin of preserved salmon, or a box of sardines, stowed away between the loaf and the jug.' The advantages of civilization were already getting to the cottager at harvest.

About 100 budgets, some estimated by the higher classes and some actually provided by cottagers themselves, can be collected from the 1893 *Report of the Royal Commission on Labour*, vol. i, and these cover practically the whole country. They are much the same as those given above. Many more for 1912 are given in Rowntree and Kendall, *How the Labourer Lives* (1913), and these, despite slight variations in quantity as between items, are composed mainly of the identical items. Tables taken from the 'Report of the Committee appointed to inquire into the financial results of the occupation of land' are provided in my *Change in Farm Labourer's Diet During Two Centuries*, printed in *Economic History* for May, 1927. None of these indicate any major change in diet.

So much for the Victorian era. It now remains to sum up the progress made by the cottager during the three centuries that have been most fertile in increasing the material wealth of the civilized world.

PART FOUR
CONCLUSIONS

CONCLUSIONS

BEFORE there was a true industrial system no man could be a helot of that system, but even under the landowning and mercantile Tudors, occasionally, the cottager had to make way for the more profitable sheep, or the enterprise of more powerful neighbours. Many cottagers, among whom at that time were numbered a large proportion of men classified, or who classified themselves, as yeomen, had the opportunity to improve their material condition, and did not fail to grasp it: but I think I should refrain from discussing the philosophical and abstract question of varying degrees of economic opportunity open to the different grades of society during some four centuries.

The Tudor period saw the beginning of the building of the modern type of two-storied cottage. The one-roomed 'house' certainly could be found in use three centuries after but, except in the North and in other very remote districts, modern standards of cottage accommodation had already been adopted by some of the best of the great landowners by the third quarter of the eighteenth century. This was some time before the so-called Industrial Revolution had got into its stride, and before the building of the 'back-to-backs' in the industrial towns of the new manufacturing districts. These 'modern' cottages were very few in the Georgian era, and many of the cottagers were housed in deplorable conditions at its end. One writer, Russell M. Garnier, however, draws a not insignificant parallel in dealing with this matter, and to a degree I subscribe to his opinion.

'Looking back on the labourer's existence at this period,' he wrote, 'one is apt to dwell unduly on its hardships and discomforts. Could the people of an earlier epoch have looked forward to it, they would probably have regarded it with envious feelings. The present nicety and decency of manners is the growth of centuries. The economy which suffered adults of both sexes to herd in one bedroom, and which did not include the commonest of modern sanitary appliances, had not begun to clash with the existent standards of either morality or health. Fifty years later public opinion had reached a pitch of refinement which revolted from the rude customs and uncouth manners of the earlier epoch. When I deal with the history of this happier period, I shall discuss the evils of the labourer's home life in far more intolerant terms than I use now. What was good enough for the "quality" in 1500 was considered good enough for the peasantry in 1800. If six labouring men and women occasionally shared the same sleeping apartment at the beginning of the nineteenth century, four times that number of the baronage class had often done so up to the beginning of the fifteenth.' He admits that the labourer of that time was worthy of less humiliating surroundings.

By 1850 very many quite reasonable cottages had been built on the great estates, but there were still many that would have been condemned as unfit for human habitation by the least progressive of modern local authorities, and Loudon's remarks made in his *Suburban Gardener and Villa Companion*, were as true then as they continued to be throughout the century. 'A thatched cottage,' he wrote, 'is an object of admiration with many persons who have not had much experience of country life.' They were, in his opinion, nearly always damp and the thatch was made pervious to the weather by the activities of cats and birds. They all harboured insects, especially earwigs and snails, and slugs from the ivy got into the kitchen because the back door was always left open. And the kitchens in low damp cottages nearly always swarmed with beetles and cockroaches and the pantry with flies, while it was almost impossible to keep fleas out of the beds. The control of all these pests is something about which a great deal was learned in the nineteenth century, and the discomforts they cause have diminished with the passage of time.[1]

Between 1850 and the end of Victoria's reign the ideal of the three-bedroomed cottage became firmly established and most of the new ones were of this type. The Report of 1893 shows that a great deal of attention was by then being paid to the details of sanitation, the purity of water supply, the disposal of waste products, and so on. There were then a good many cottages, survivals of an earlier age, some of which, especially in the North, were of the one-room or two-ended type and

[1] Yet some 11 per cent of children evacuated from town to country in 1939-40 were verminous. *See* Cyril Falls, *The Second World War*. 1948.

some of which had only one up and one down, and such survivals have not completely vanished to-day, if Francis Brett Young's fictional sketch of housing in an imaginary West Midland Village quoted in *The English Scene*, is accepted. Supported as it is by Reginald Arkell's statement in *A Cottage in the Country* (1934), that he visited a 'lovely valley where, with my own eyes, I saw the legs of three bedsteads coming through the ceilings of three separate kitchens', and by H. J. Massingham's *Country* (1934) where he says, underlining Loudon of nearly a century before, 'I should like to take a party of these high-minded æsthetes into the interiors of some of our older thatched cottages in the village [in Buckinghamshire]. In one it would find eight human beings sleeping in one room, the parents and six children. It looks very nice, that cottage. In another of these pretty little cottages lived a woman and her husband with three children. She became pregnant once more, and the birth took place in the one bedroom for five people. The only other room was the sitting den. . . .'

Unfortunately there is no means, as I have pointed out already, of knowing what proportion of such survivals continued to be occupied up to the turn of the century and after. That there were some is evident, but it may be that it was by being uncommon that they caused so much remark by modern writers—with an urban outlook. It is quite certain that in many parts of the great towns there was equal overcrowding at the same date, and there is no doubt at all that from the middle of the eighteenth century improved cottages, with a scale of accommodation, except plumbing, not very far removed from that of the modern urban five- or six-roomed villas, had been built in numbers. It is equally evident that not enough were built and that many of the labourers continued, not to put too fine a point upon it, to be inadequately housed.

Furniture and clothing in the Tudor period were of the simplest, and often the low standards of the day were not reached. Clothes were of a kind that were expected to last a lifetime, a Stuart vicar being almost surprised that he was at last compelled to have a new cassock after wearing the old one for thirty-five years. The new one was, of course, nothing like the quality of the old. The interiors of the cottages were provided with only the simplest effects, often home made, if not the results of the skill of the village carpenter, and in number limited to the smallest modicum. As the centuries passed and the substantial leather and fustian went into disuse, clothing had to be replaced more frequently, although the wedding garment continued to serve as Sunday wear for a lifetime. The women and children of the modern time were often clad in the made over cast-offs of the better-off villagers. Boots and shoes were always a problem, for the man must have his repaired, and an occasional new pair to replace those irretrievably worn out. Furniture and clothing, like housing, for many of the villagers remained at an almost inconceivably low level throughout the centuries, and it would be difficult to say that the cottager was in any measurable degree better off in Victorian than he was in Tudor times. The things he used were different, but generally speaking not more ample; but like the houses themselves the contents varied and many cottagers in spite of their limited accommodation and simple effects were doubtless comfortable in the sense in which they understood the word: but there is no shadow of doubt that they lived on the minimum necessities, whatever their circumstances, to which the word can in any real sense be applied.

There are more precise details of the food, both in kind and quantity, on which the cottagers managed to sustain life. The items comprised in the regimen hardly changed in the four centuries under review. At the end of the period only wheaten bread was eaten, but until well into the nineteenth century several other cereals, notably barley as well as oats, though perhaps not so much rye, were used, and some legumes, like pea and bean flour, in bad times. During much of the winter the rich were poorly fed in Tudor times. The methods of meat preservation in use, salting and smoking, did not fully preserve these stores for the whole period, and what there was of this preserved meat (there was little or no fresh meat eaten at this time of the year) became more and more unpalatable, nay unwholesome, as the winter advanced towards the spring. When the rich were so hard up, the poor could hardly be less so, and meat in any form could not have graced their tables at this time of the year. Indeed it is unlikely that a meat meal was of more frequent occurrence than once a week, and that was probably pig-meat, although larger quantities were likely to have been eaten by each participant at this one meal than is customary in the modern world. Conditions of meat consumption did not change very much from that time until the Victorian era, but in that era the use of the potato, a food much condemned by Cobbett, although doubtless fairly generally eaten in his day, became widespread. In many counties the farmer provided the ground, ploughed and manured it, and so gave the labourer a useful and practically costless supplement to his normal

'lenten' feast. So early as 1863 the average consumption of this veget-
able by the cottage class is estimated to have been some 7 lb. a week
each.

Another point is worthy of comment, although perhaps not very
important. In the early part of the eighteenth century, and for centuries
before, a very light beer was the common drink. It was distributed in
the eighteenth century to poor-houses at the rate of 1 pint a meal or
1 quart a day, and it figured in the diet of the labourers of the north as
well as in the south, although the former were in the habit of using
milk with their porridge. This light beer had disappeared from the
budget of the labourer by the end of the eighteenth century—I will
not say that none was drank by him—and in modern times a
smaller quantity of milk than was formerly used took its place.
This small quantity of milk was presumably used with the almost
minute quantities of tea and cocoa that find a place in the recorded
budgets.

The opportunities which living in the country provide for adding
to the purchased foodstuffs, by catching rabbits and winged game,
either legally or by poaching, and in some districts by legal or illegal
fishing, must not be overlooked; nor the fact that the cottager in some
places had a garden in which fresh vegetables could be grown and an
occasional fruit tree flourished, but in many ways the advantages which
have accrued to an urban civilization seem to have passed over the
head of the agricultural labourer. This is not to say that he was any
worse off than many of his prototypes in the industrial towns. He
doubtless often thought that he was and acted accordingly, but on the
lowest levels of urban employment there were conditions certainly no
better, and often much worse, than those in which the countryman
lived. In spite of the elementary nature of much rural sanitation, the
atmosphere was not wholly polluted, and it must be remembered that
in many towns up to the turn of the nineteenth century and later
there was still no system of water-borne sewage disposal.

Many people have added to this advantage the contention that the
countryman was happier than the townsman, in spite of the hardness of
his lot, because his work was a direct struggle to overcome the forces
of nature, and he was less tempted to look upon himself as a mere cog
in the wheel than the modern factory operative. He has, indeed, a satisfaction in his work that is so lacking in many urban occupations that
the townsman feels himself properly alive and seeks his happiness
only when he is released from his factory bench or office stool: but

I cannot do better than conclude by quoting *Medieval Panorama* (1938), by G. G. Coulton, who says: 'This, however, is often exaggerated beyònd all reason by modern writers, who do not themselves grapple with nature...', and add that I can only agree with this depreciation of what is often mere rhetorical flourishing, combined with a definitely fetishistic view of life in the country.

PRICES

The prices are all food prices. The wages of the agricultural labourer were largely spent on food. Grain or bread was by far the most important purchase, taking, even in prosperous times, between 30 per cent. and 70 per cent. of the total wage. Meat was often outside the purchasing power of the labourer.

PART I (1485–1714)

Wages of a day labourer: early 17th century, about 6d. a day.

   ,, ,, ,, ,,   ,,   late 17th century, 8d. to 10d. a day.

Average price of grain, per qtr.	*Wheat*	*Barley*	*Oats*
in 1601–10 .	32s. 6d.	16s. 10d.	10s. 6d.
in 1691–1700	36s. 0d.	22s. 0d.	14s. 0d.

(Prices were higher during the Civil War)

Average price of a cow: *c.* 1600, about £3.

PART II (1714–1837)

Wages of a day labourer: *c.* 1700, 10d.–1s. 0d. a day.

   ,,   ,, ,, ,,   ,,   *c.* 1837, 7s. to 9s. a week.

Average price of grain, per qtr.	*Wheat*	*Barley*	*Oats*
in 1790	56s. 0d.	*c.* 25s. 0d.	*c.* 19s. 0d.
in 1801–10	83s. 0d.		
in 1810–13	106s. 0d.		

Average price of butter: late eighteenth century, 9d. lb.

   ,,   ,,   ,, bacon: ,,   ,,   ,,   3d. lb.

   ,,   ,,   ,, a cow: ,,   ,,   ,,   £8 and upwards.

PART III (1837–1901)

Average wages of a day labourer rose slowly, with fluctuations, to about 12s. and 14s. a week towards 1914.

Average prices, mid-nineteenth century: Wheat, 50s. to 60s. qtr.

   ,,   ,,   ,,   ,,   Potatoes, *c.* ½d. lb.

   ,,   ,,   ,,   ,,   Butter, 9d. to 1s. 0d. lb.

   ,,   ,,   ,,   ,,   Meat, 6d. lb.

   ,,   ,,   in 1900:   Bread, 5d. to 6d. 4lb. loaf.

   ,,   ,,   ,,   Butter, 1s. 0d. to 1s. 4d. lb.

   ,,   ,,   ,,   A cow, £20 to £25.

For purpose of comparison it may be noted that the average minimum agricultural wage in 1938–39 was about 34s. a week. The price of Bread was 9d. 4lb. loaf; of Butter about 1s. 2d. to 1s. 6d. lb.; of Margarine about 4d. to 8d. lb.

INDEX.

BIBLIOGRAPHY

I. GOVERNMENT PUBLICATIONS

Employment of Women and Children in Agriculture, 1843 (Report of Royal Commission).

Employment of Children, 1867 (Royal Commission).

Labour, Royal Commission on, 1893.

Rural Cottages, Report of the Advisory Committee on, 1911.

Select Committee of the House of Lords on the State of Agriculture, 1836.

II. CONTEMPORARY WORKS

An Historical Account of Mr. Roger's Three Years Travels over England and Wales, 1694.

Annals of Agriculture, 1783 et seq.

Anon, *An Account of Several Workhouses for employing and maintaining the Poor*, 1725.

Anon, *North of Scotland and England in MDCCIV*, 1818.

Anon, *Rural Elegance Displayed*, 1768.

Anon, *Universal Dictionary of Trade and Commerce*, 1775.

Author of *A Tour in Ireland. Journal of a Tour to the Western Counties in 1807,1809*.

Bailey, John, *Gen. View. Agric. Durham*, 1810.

—, and Culley, G., *Gen. View. Agric. Northumberland*, 1797.

—, —, *Gen. View. Agric. Cumberland*, 1794.

—, —, *Gen. View. Agric. Cumberland*, 1797.

Beatson, Robert, *On Farm Buildings in General. Communications to the Board of Agric.* (1797), vol. i, and other contributions on this subject therein.

Billingsley, J., *Gen. View. Agric. Somerset*, 1798.

Bloomfield, Robert, *The Farmer's Boy*, 1800.

Brontë, Emily, *Wuthering Heights*, 1847.

Brown, Thomas, *Gen. View. Agric. Derby*, 1794.

Brown, W., *Gen. View. Agric. West Riding*, 1799.

Burritt, Elihu, *A Walk from London to Land's End and Back*, 1865.

Butcher, Rev. Edmund, *An Excursion from Sidmouth to Chester . . . in* 1803, 1805.

Caird, James, *English Agriculture in* 1850–1, 1852.

Carew of Anthonie, Cornwall, Richard, *Survey of Cornwall*, 1602.

Clare, John, *Poems, Descriptive of Rural Life and Scenery*, 1820.

Claridge, John, *Gen. View. Agric. Dorset*, 1793.

Clark, John, *Gen. View. Agric. Hereford*, 1794.

Clarke, Edward Daniel, *A Tour through the South of England. Wales . . .* 1791, 1793.

Clifford, Frederick, *The Agricultural Lock-out of* 1874, 1875.

Climenson, Emily J., (ed.) *Passages from the Diaries of Mrs. Philip Lybbe Powys*, 1899.

Cobbett, William, *Twopenny Trash*, 1831.

—, *Rural Rides* (ed. by Pitt Cobbet), 1893.

Cobbold, Richard, *Margaret Catchpole*, 1845.

Cowper, William, *The Task*, 1785.

Crabbe, Rev. George, *The Village*, 1783.

Crutwell, Rev. C., *Tour through Great Britain*, 1801.

Davies, Rev. J., *Case of the Labourers in Husbandry*, 1795.

Davis, Thomas, *Address to the Landholders of the Kingdom . . .*, 1795 (Letters and Com. to the Bath and West Soc. vii).

—, *Gen. View. Agric. Wiltshire*, 1813.

Dennis, Alexander, *Journal of a Tour . . . in . . .* 1810, 1816.

Dickson and Stevenson, *Gen. View. Agric. Lancashire*, 1815.

Dictionarium Rusticum, 1704.

Donaldson, James, *Gen. View. Agric. Northampton*, 1794.

Doncaster Gazette, 21st March, 1842.

Duncombe, John, *Gen. View. Agric. Hereford*, 1805.

Dunsford, M., *Historical Memoirs of the Town and Parish of Tiverton*, 1790.

Dyer, John, *The Fleece*, 1757.

Eden, Sir Frederick, *State of the Poor*, 1797, 2 vols.

Eliot, George, *Scenes of Clerical Life*, 1857.

—, *Adam Bede*, 1859.

Ellis, William, *Chiltern and Vale Farming Explained*, 1733.

Farey, William, *Gen. View. Agric. Derby*, 1815.

Fielding, Henry, *Tom Jones*, 1749.

—, *Joseph Andrews*, 1742.

Forster, John, *England's Happiness Increased: or a sure and easy Remedy against all succeeding Dear Years; by a Plantation of the Roots called Potatoes*, 1664.

Fraser, R., *Gen. View. Agric. Devon*, 1794.

—, *Gen. View. Agric. Cornwall*, 1794.

Gay, John, *Shepherds Week*, 1714.
Gentleman, A, *A Tour from London to the Lakes in* . . . 1791, 1792.
Gilpin, Rev. William, *Remarks on Forest Scenery*, 1791.
Goldsmith, Oliver, *The Vicar of Wakefield*, 1766.
Gooch, W., *Gen. View. Agric. Cambridge*, 1813.

Harrison's *Description of England in Shakespeare's Youth*, 1877, ed. by Fredk. J. Furnivall.
Hassell, J. A., *Tour in the Isle of Wight*, 1790 (Pinkerton's Tours).
Hayden, E. C., *Travels round our Village*, 1905.
Heath, F. G., *The English Peasantry*, 1874.
Heath, Richard, *The English Peasant*, 1872.
Holdenby, Christopher, *The Folk of the Furrow*, 1913.
Holland, Henry, *Gen. View. Agric. Cheshire*, 1808.
Housman, John, *Topographical Description of Cumberland, etc.*, 1800.
Howitt, William, *The Rural Life of England*, 1838, 2 vols.
Hudson, W. H., *A Shepherd's Life*, ed. of 1926.
—, *Hampshire Days*, 1923.
Hughes, Thomas, *Tom Brown's Schooldays*, 1856.
—, *The Scouring of the White Horse*, 1858.
Hutchinson, W., *View of Northumberland, Anno* 1776, 1778.
—, *An Excursion to the Lakes* . . . *August:* 1773, 1774.
Hutton, John, *A Tour to the Caves* . . . *and* . . . *Ingleborough*, 1781, 2nd ed.
Hutton, W., *History of Derby*, 1791.

James, William, and Malcolm, James, *General view of the Agric.* . . . *of Buckingham*, 1794.
Jefferies, Richard, *Round about a Great Estate*, 1880 and other works.
Jessopp, Rev. Augustus, *Arcady for Better or Worse*, 1887.
Johnson, C. W., and Cressy, Ed., *The Cottages of Agricultural Labourers*, 1847.
Johnson, Samuel, *A Diary of a Journey into North Wales in* . . . 1774, 1816.

Kalm, Pehr, *Kalm's Account of his Visit to England on his way to America in* 1748, 1892, tr. by Joseph Lucas.
Kebbel, T. E., *The old and the new English Country Life*, 1891.
—, *The Agricultural Labourer*, 1907, 4th ed.
Kent, Nathaniel, *Hints to Gentlemen of Landed Property*, 1775.
Kilmansegge, Count Frederick, *Diary of a Journey to England in* 1761–62, 1902. Tr. by Countess Kilmansegge.
Kingsley, Charles, *Alton Locke*, 1849.
—, *Yeast*, 1851.

Laing, D., *Hints for Dwellings*, 1800.
A Landowner, *Rural Improvements*, 1775.
Laurence, Edward, *The Duty of a Steward to his Lord*, 1727.

[Lawrence, John], *The Modern Land Steward*, 1801.
Leatham, J., *Gen. View. Agric. East Riding*, 1794.
Lipscombe, George, *A Journey into Cornwall*, 1799.
Loudon, J. C., *Suburban Gardener and Villa Companion*, 1838.

MacRitchie, Rev. Wm., *Diary of a Tour through Great Britain in 1795*, 1897.
Manners, John, Duke of Rutland, *Journals of Three Years' Travels* ... 1795-7, 1805.
Marshall, William, *Rural Economy of the West of England*, 1796.
—, *Rural Economy of the Southern Counties*, 1798.
—, *Rural Economy of the Midlands*, 1790.
—, *Rural Economy of Yorkshire*, 1788.
—, *Rural Economy of Gloucestershire*, 1807.
Maton, William George, *Observations on the Western Counties*, 1794 *and* 1796, 1797.
Mavor, William, *Gen. View. Agric. Berkshire*, 1808.
M'Phail, James, *A Treatise on the Culture of the Cucumber*, 1794.
Miller, J., *The Country Gentleman's Architect*, 1787.
M. Misson's *Memoirs and Observations in his Travels over England*, 1719 (Tr. by Mr. Ozell).
Mitford, Mary, *Our Village*, 1824.
Monk, John, *Gen. View. Agric. Leicester*, 1794.
Mordant, John, *The Compleat Steward*, 1761.
Morton, John C., *Cyclopædia of Agriculture*, 1856.
Moryson, Fynes, *An Itinerary*. . . , 1617.
Muralt, Beat. Louis De, *Letters describing the Character and Customs of the English and French Nations*, 1726.
Murray, Adam, *Gen. View. Agric. Warwick*, 1813.

O'Neill, Hugh, *Devonshire Idylls*, 1892.

Parkinson, Richard, *Gen. View. Agric. Rutland*, 1808.
P[atching], R[esta], *Four topographical letters written in July, 1755* (1757).
Pearce, William, *Gen. View. Agric. Berkshire*, 1794.
Pennant, Thomas, *A Journey from London to the Isle of Wight*, 1801.
Pitt, W., *Gen. View. Agric. Northampton*, 1809.
—, *Gen. View. Agric. Stafford*, 1808.
—, *Gen. View. Agric. Leicester*, 1808.
—, *Gen. View. Agric. Worcester*, 1813.
Plat, Sir Hugh, *Sundrie New and Artificial Remedies against Famine* . . ., 1596.
Plaw, John, *Rural Architecture*, 1794.
—, *Sketches of Country Houses*, 1800.
Plymley, Joseph, *Gen. View. Agric. Shropshire*, 1803.
Pococke, Dr., *Travels through England*. Camden Soc. N.S. xliv.

Pomeroy, W. T., *Gen. View. Agric. Worcester*, 1794.

Postans, Thomas, *A letter to Sir Thomas Baring, Bart. . . . on the causes . . . produced the present state of the Agricultural Labouring Poor*, 1831.

Powicke, F. G., (ed.), *The Rev. Richard Baxter's Last Treatise*, 1691.

Pratt, S. J., *Gleanings in England*, 1799.

Present State of England, 1750.

Priest, Rev. St. John, *Gen. View. Agric. Buckingham*, 1813.

Q[uincy], T[homas], *A short tour of the Midland Counties . . . in 1772, 1774. 1775.*

Reasons for the late increase in the Poor Rates, 1777.

Rennie, Brown and Sherriff, *Gen. View. Agric. West Riding*, 1794.

Richardson, C. J., *The Englishman's House*, 1870.

Rigby, Edward, *Reports of the Special Provision Committee appointed . . . Norwich* 1788.

Roberts, Mary, *Annals of My Village*, 1831.

Roland, Jeanne-Marie Philipson, *Works*, 1800.

Rudge, Thomas, *Gen. View. Agric. Gloucestershire*, 1807.

Shaw, Rev. Stebbing, *A Tour of the West of England in 1788, 1789.*

Shenstone, Wm., *Poems, c. 1745.*

Simond, L., *Journal of a tour and residence in Great Britain by a French traveller*, 1815.

Smollet, Tobias, *The Adventures of Sir Launcelot Greaves*, 1760.

Soane, Sir John, *Sketches in Architecture*, 1793.

Somerville, Alexander, *The Whistler at the Plough*, 1852.

Stevenson, William, *Gen. View. Agric. Sussex*, 1809.

—, *Gen. View. Agric. Dorset*, 1812.

Taine, Henri, *Notes on England* (ed. of), 1876.

Taylor, John, the water poet, *A discovery by sea from London to Salisbury*, 1623, and other works.

Thornton, Col. T., *A Sporting Tour . . . North of England*, 1804.

Tuckwell, Rev. Canon, *Reminiscences of a Radical Parson*, 1895.

Tuke, Mr., *Gen. View. Agric. North Riding*, 1794.

Tusser, Thomas, *Five hundred points of good husbandry*, 1577.

—, *One hundred points of . . .*, 1557.

Vancouver, Chas., *Gen. View. Agric. Hampshire*, 1813.

Wedge, John, *Gen. View. Agric. Warwick*, 1794.

—, *Gen. View. Agric. Cheshire*, 1794.

White, Gilbert, *Natural History of Selborne.*

White, Walter, *A Londoner's Walk to Land's End*, 1855.

Wigstead, Henry, *Remarks on a tour through North and South Wales made in the year 1797.*

Wood, John, *A series of plans for cottages*, new ed., 1792.
Worgan, G. B., *Gen. View. Agric. Cornwall*, 1811.
Wyndham, H. P., *A picture of the Isle of Wight in the year* 1793, 1794.

Young, Arthur, *A Six Months' Tour through the North of England*, 2nd ed.
—, *Gen. View. Agric. Suffolk*, 1797.
—, *Gen. View. Agric. Lincoln*, 1799.
—, *Gen. View. Agric. Essex*, 1807.
Young, Rev. Arthur, *Gen. View. Agric. Sussex*, 1808.

III. MODERN WORKS

Addy, S. O., *The Evolution of the English House*, 1898.
Allsopp, H., *The Change to Modern England*, 1922.
Arch, Joseph, *The Story of His.Life told by Himself*, 1898.
Arkell, Reginald, *A Cottage in the Country*, 1934.
Ashley, W. J., *The Bread of our Forefathers*, 1928.
Atkinson, D. H., *Ralph Thoresby, the Topographer; his Town and his Times*, 1885
Atkinson, Rev. J. C., *Forty Years in a Moorland Parish*, 1891.

Baldry, George, *The Rabbit Skin Cap* (ed. by Lilias Rider Haggard), 1939.
Barfield, S., *Thatcham: Berks., and its Manors*, 1901.
Barnes, William, *Poems in the Dorset Dialect*, 1863.
Barnett, Herbert, *Glupton, the History of an Oxfordshire Manor*, 1923 (Oxford Record Soc.), vol. v.
Batsford, Harry, and Fry, Charles, *The English Cottage*, 1938.
Bennett, E. N., *Problems of Village Life*, n.d. (*c.* 1913).
Best, Henry, *Farming and Account Books*, 1641, in Surtees Soc., vol. 33, 1857.
Blackmore, Richard D., *Lorna Doone*, 1869.
—, *Cripps the Carrier*, 1876.
Blomefield, J. C., *History of Finmere, Oxon.*, 1887.
Bradford Antiquary (a periodical publication).
Bradley, A. G., *Round about Wiltshire*, 1907.
—, *Exmoor Memoirs*, 1926.

Clapham, J. H. (Sir John), *An Economic History of Modern Britain*, 1926, 3 vols.
Clark, Atwood, *Country Mixture*, 1934.
Cornwall, *Royal Institution Journal*.
Coulton, G. G., *Medieval Panorama*, 1938.
Cox, Rev. J. Chas., *Three Centuries of Derbyshire Annals*, 1890.
—, *Churchwardens' Accounts*, 1913.
Crossing, William, *A Hundred Years on Dartmoor*, 1902.
Cumberland and Westmorland Antiquarian Soc. Trans.

Darby, H. C., *Historical Geography of England before* 1800, 1936.
Davies, Godfrey, *The Early Stuarts*, 1603–60, 1937.
Derbyshire Archæological and Natural History Society (Annual Journal).
Devon Association Transactions.
Devonshire Association, *Parochial Histories of the County of Devon*, 1932, vols. i–iv
    et seq.
Drummond, J. C., and Wilbraham Anne, *The Englishman's Food*, 1939.

Ellis, Clough Williams, *Cottage Building in Cob, Pisé, Chalk and Clay*, 1919.
Ernle, Lord, *The Land and its People*, 1925.
—, *English Farming Past and Present*, 1932.

Farrer, William, *The Court Rolls of the Honour of Clitheroe in the County of
    Lancaster*, 1879, 3 vols.
Finch, William Coles, *Life in Rural England*, n.d. (c. 1890).
Firebrace, Cordell William, *Honest Harry. Being the Biography of Sir Henry
    Firebrace, Kt.:* 1619–91, 1932.
Fletcher, J. S., *Memoirs of a Yorkshire Parish* (Darrington), 1917.
Francis, M. E., *In a North Country Village*, 1896.
Fussell, G. E., *Change in Farm Labourer's Diet during two Centuries*, in *Econ.
    Hist.*, May, 1927.
—, *Rural Housing in the eighteenth century*, ibid., 1930.
—, *Social and Agrarian Background of the Pilgrim Fathers* in *Agricultural History*,
    October, 1933.
—, *Farming methods in the early Stuart period* in *Journal of Modern History*, 1935.
—, *Pioneer farming in the late Stuart age* in *Journal* of R.A. S. E., 1940.
—, *Dawn of High Farming in England* in *Agricultural History*, 1948.
—, *High Farming* in *Economic Geography*, 1948 *et seq.*
—, *Steam Cultivation in England* in *Engineering*, July and August, 1943.

Garnier, Russell M., *Annals of the British Peasantry*, 1895.
George, M. Dorothy, *England in Transition*, 1931.
Gilboy, Elizabeth W., *Wages in Eighteenth Century England*, 1934.
Gould, S. Baring, *A Book of the West*, 1899.
Green, F. E., *A History of the English Agricultural Labourer* (1870–1920), 1920.
Green, J. L., *English Country Cottages*, n.d. (c. 1914).

Halévy, Elie, *A History of the English People in* 1815, 1924.
Halsham, John, *Idlehurst*, 1897.
Hamlyn, F. C., *A History of Morwenstowe after the Restoration*, 1930.
Hammond, J. L., and Barbara, *The Village Labourer*, 1911.
Hampson, E. M., *The Treatment of Poverty in Cambridgeshire* (1597–1834), 1934.

Hasbach, W., *History of the English Agricultural Labourer*, 1908 (tr. by Ruth Kenyon).

Hoskyns, C. W., *The Leicestershire Farmer in the sixteenth century*, 1941–2, *Trans. Leics. Arch. Soc.*

Humphreys, A. L., *Bucklebury, a Berkshire Parish*, 1932.

Hussey, Christopher, *The Picturesque*, 1927.

Innocent, G. F., *The Development of English Building Construction*, 1916.

Jekyll, Gertrude, *Old English Household Life*, 1925.

Jenkin, A. K. Hamilton, *Cornwall and its People*, 1945 (*Cornish Homes and Customs*, 1934, is included in the above).

Jones, Evan J., *Some Contributions to the Economic History of Wales*, 1928.

Lambert, A. U. M., *Godstone, a Parish History*, 1929.

Lambert, Sir H. C. M., *History of Banstead in Surrey*, 1912.

Lambert, Uvedale, *Blechingley, a Parish History*, 1921.

Lee, Sir Sidney, (ed.), *Shakespeare's England*, 1916. *Agriculture and Gardening*, by R. E. Prothero (Lord Ernle).

Lennard, Reginald, *English agriculture in the reign of Charles II* in *Economic History Review*. October 1932.

Lewis, Wyndham, *Mysterious Mr. Bull*, 1938.

Massingham, H. G., *Country*, 1934.

Mercer, W. B., *Thomas Furber, an eighteenth cent. Cheesemaker*, 1933 (Reaseheath Review, vol. v).

Merritt, Anna Lee, *A Hamlet in Old Hampshire*, 1902.

Meynell, Esther, *Country Ways*, 1942.

Middleton, C. H., *Village Memories*, 1941.

Midland Record Society Publications, 1896 *et seq.*

Moffitt, Louis W., *England on the eve of the Industrial Revolution*, 1925.

Mosshead, J. Y. A., *A History of Salcombe Regis*, 1898. *Trans. Devon Assn.*, vol. xxx.

Orlebar, Frederica St. John, *The Orlebar Chronicles in Bedfordshire and Northampton*, 1930.

Orwin, C. S., *Agriculture and Rural Life* in *Johnson's England*: 1933 (ed., A. S. Turbeville).

Palmer, W. N., *Meldreth Parish Records*, 1896.

Penney, Norman, (ed.) *The Household Account Book of Sarah Fell*, 1920.

A. H. Plaisted, *The manor and parish records of Medmenham, Bucks*, 1925.

—, *The parson and parish registers of Medmenham, Bucks*, 1932.

Powys, Llewellyn, *Dorset Essays*, 1935.
—, *Somerset Essays*, 1937.

Robinson, Maude, *A Southdown Farm in the Sixties*, 1938.
Rowntree, Seebohm, and Kendall, May, *How the Labourer Lives*, 1913.
Royal Agricultural Society Journal, 1839 *et seq.*

Sayce, R. U., *Popular enclosures and the one night house* in *Collec. Histl. and Arch. Montgomeryshire*, xlviii (1942), pt. ii.
Springall, L. Marion, *Labouring Life in Norfolk Villages*, 1834–1914. 1936.
Stearns, Raymond Phineas, *Agricultural Adaptation in England*, 1875–1900 in *Agricultural History*, 1932.
Surrey Archæological Collections (ann) 1858–1919.
Surtees Soc. Publications—especially the Wills and Inventories Series.

Tait, James, ed. *Lancashire Quarter Sessions Records*. Chetham Soc., vol. 77 N.S., 1917.
Tawney, R. H., *The Agrarian Problem in the sixteenth century*, 1912.
Thomas, Edward, *The Heart of England*, 1909.
Tough, D. W., *The last years of a frontier. A history of the Borders during the reign of Elizabeth*, 1928.
Trevelyan, G. M., *England under the Stuarts*, 1904.
Tupling, G. H., *The economic history of Rossendale*, 1927.

Warren, C. Henry, *The Happy Countryman*, 1939.
Williams, Alfred, *Folk Songs of the Upper Thames*, 1923.
—, *Round About the Upper Thames*, 1922.
—, *A Wiltshire Village*, 1912.
Wiltshire Archæological and Nat. Hist. Mag., 1876 *et seq.*

Young, Francis Brett, *Portrait of a Village*, quoted in F. A. Walbank, *The English Scene*.
Young, G. M., *Early Victorian England:* 1830–65, 1934.

FURTHER READING

In addition to the works cited in Section III of the above bibliography, there are several that deal with the general social history of the period, the more important being:

Trevelyan, G. M., *English Social History*, 1944.
Black, J. B., *The reign of Elizabeth*, 1936.
Davis, Godfrey, *The Early Stuarts*, 1937.
Clark, G. N., *The Later Stuarts*, 1934.
Ensor, R. C., *England, 1870–1914*, 1936.
Hamilton, Henry, *History of the Homeland*, 1947.